# SHOW UP

## NA'IMA B. ROBERT

# A Motivational Message for Muslim Women

**KUBE**
PUBLISHING

*Show Up: A Motivational Message for Muslim Women*

*First Published in England by*
Kube Publishing Ltd
MCC, Ratby Lane, Markfield
Leicestershire, LE67 9SY
United Kingdom
Tel: +44 (0) 1530 249230
Email: info@kubepublishing.com
Website: www.kubepublishing.com

CIP data for this book is available from the British Library.

ISBN: 978-1-84774-148-6 *casebound*
ISBN: 978-1-84774-141-7 *paperback*
ISBN: 978-1-84774-142-4 *ebook*

*Editor*: Asma Anwar
*Cover Design*: Jannah Haque
*Typesetting*: Nasir Cadir
*Printed by*: Elma Basım, Turkey

# Contents

Introduction ✳ 1

1

The Loss ✳ 5

2

WHAT is 'Showing Up'? ✳ 15
Showing up: A Prophetic Sunnah ✳ 20

3

What does 'Showing Up' in YOUR life look like? ✳ 25
Showing up for yourself ✳ 28
Showing up for your relationship ✳ 30

Showing up for your children ✳ 31
Showing up for your family ✳ 32
Showing up for your dreams ✳ 32
Circle of influence ✳ 33


4

The HOW of 'Showing Up' ✳ 37
Step One: Be Intentional ✳ 41
Step Two: Be Positive ✳ 49
Step Three: Cultivate Gratitude ✳ 61
Step Four: Have Courage ✳ 65
Step Five: Embrace Flow ✳ 78
Step Six: Be You! ✳ 91


In Conclusion ✳ 109


Acknowledgements ✳ 113


Appendix: Bonus Material ✳ 115


Bibliography ✳ 119

# Endorsements

"Na'ima brings out our dynamism by letting us see her (usually invisible) fragility. I was crying by page ten and ready to take on the world a chapter later! This is a boost in times of global fear and personal challenges!"

**Lauren Booth**, Author '*Finding Peace in the Holy Land*' and '*Accidentally Muslim*'

"I was so overwhelmed with emotion and started sobbing three pages in. I appreciate Na'ima sharing a love story that will – insha Allah – continue in the heavens above."

**Selina Bakkar**, Founder, Amaliah

"Through a deeply personal narrative of her own journey after the death of her husband, Na'ima B. Robert inspires Muslim women to gather the resources available to them so they can be the heroine in their stories and show up as victors. '*Show Up*' is a powerful testimony of the beauty that's possible when you choose to rise in the face of life's challenges as a heroine in your life story."

**LaYinka Sanni**, Host, Honest Tea Talk

"I read '*Show Up*' in exactly 3 hours! When I decided to read it the morning I received it, my intention was just to get started, however, the writing style was so beautiful, the message so straight to the point and the actionable takeaways were so clearly outlined, I couldn't stop.

It's about time someone gave us the wake up call! And who better than one who is already living the truth she is inviting others to?"

**Aishah Adams**, Author, '*Rise, Irrespective*'
CEO, The Support Lounge

"Finally. Finally a motivational self-help, self-care book written for the Muslim woman, with Islamic references and stories intricately woven in. This gives it beautiful depth. Na'ima B. Robert has written an insightful book, full of raw vulnerability, sharing her own deeply personal stories and experiences. This book reads like a love-letter to the sisterhood of Muslim women to inspire her to "...*choose courage over fear*". It takes the reader on a reflective journey that lights a fire of hope for whichever life stage she's at, and for situations she has faced or is facing. It guides her on how to 'show up' authentically with an easy to follow, step-by-step process. This is a must-read for any Muslim woman ready to be present as a hero in her life, and for any woman trying to find the courage to do so." As Robert asks "*Now is the time for it, if not now, then when? And, if not you, then who?*".

**Tumkeen**, Writer and Poet,
*Contributing Writer for Detroit Mom and Lansing Mom*

Bismillahir-Rahmanir-Raheem

# Introduction

**It came as a shock.**

**I found him unconscious on the bed early
on Saturday morning and, within two weeks,
he was gone.**

**A shock.
An out-of-the-blue, out of nowhere,
blindsiding shock.**

\*\*\*

I dedicated my first major book, *'From My Sisters' Lips'*, to my husband, Sulayman Henry Amankwah. The dedication read:

*For my husband, the wind beneath my wings.*

Even now, I look back and marvel at how fitting that dedication was.

We married young, young enough to make both our families feel uncomfortable. They were convinced that we weren't ready for the responsibilities of married life, that we should wait a few more years, get 'established', be 'sure'.

But we were sure.

And we handled it.

I remember our early years together as the adventure story of two kids: two eager, fairly new Muslims, playing House. He went out to work, I stayed home and cooked (badly); and dressed up before he got home. When I worked in East London, he used to drive all the way over from Northwest to drop me off at Whitechapel. This was so that I wouldn't have to take the train on my own at night. Or maybe he just wanted to be with me.

We developed our own rituals as a young couple: travelling to Watford every Monday to attend Islamic talks held in a friend's house, visiting his mother on the weekend, staying up late on Saturday nights to talk and laugh and laugh and laugh.

Then our first baby came and we shifted gears: we were parents.

I will never forget my first labour: it was at home, Sulayman was in attendance, calm and supportive, and my sister was cooking upstairs. I gave birth naturally, in the bath, then we all ate rice and chicken together. That night, the baby wouldn't settle for the longest time and I was ready to crash out, exhausted. Sulayman lay at the end of our mattress on the floor, his body curled around the baby, soothing him until he fell asleep.

He never lost that touch.

We had four more children after that, alhamdulillah, three of them in different homes, in different countries, and one in hospital. We explored different careers: he went from selling websites to small businesses, to setting up a mobile phone company and finally a call centre in Egypt. I went from teaching, to setting up a school in my front room, to writing and doing henna as a profession, to writing full-time, to setting up a magazine called SISTERS.

When our third child was one, we decided to leave the UK and settle in Egypt for the children to have easier access to the Arabic language and to learn the Qur'an. We lived a good life there, surrounded by friends who had moved for similar reasons. We performed hajj and decided to take the leap into homeschooling.

Quite simply, we understood each other, we supported each other, we were best friends and allies, as well as husband and wife. It is no exaggeration to say that, without him, I would not be the woman I am today.

Sulayman's understanding and patient attitude brought out the best in me, in deen and dunyah. His way was not to command or force, but rather advise and let me make my own mistakes and learn from them. As with those he worked with, his aim was always to support me in fulfilling my potential, because it was that quality that had drawn him to me in the first place (his words, not mine!).

So, how did I find myself in 2016, a single mother of five children, CEO of a business I didn't know, facing an unknown and unknowable future?

In this book, I will be sharing with you the story of how I came to understand the meaning of 'Showing Up' through tragic circumstances and enormous life changes. I will also share the roadmap I used to come back from the brink of despair to a life of contribution and meaning, and the ideas and insights I have gleaned over the years, inspired by the Qur'an and Sunnah and by the many teachers and mentors I have had during this time, alhamdulillah.

Throughout the book, I invite you to pause and reflect on the ideas I share, to answer questions about your own life situation and, piece by piece, build your own roadmap towards showing up as the hero of your life story.

Feel free to mark the pages, write notes and use the space provided to make this book a transformational, healing journey that is personal and pertinent to you.

To help you, I have created a free workbook that you can download and use as you read through this book. I pray that it helps you get the clarity and insight you need to start on your own 'Show Up' journey.

Download the workbook here:

**www.naimarobert.com/showup**

# 1

# The Loss

At the end of our fourteenth year together, my husband and I decided to go for 'umrah with the kids. We hoped that it would be another beautiful holiday together, combining family time with worship. But even today, I see that trip as the starting point of the downward spiral.

Sulayman became ill and tensions were rising between him and our eldest child. Their relationship fractured, almost beyond repair, it seemed, and I could see that it was weighing on him. Weakened now, work issues also began to take their toll on him. I had never seen him that ill at ease, that agitated.

One evening, I went out to eat with a sister and left him at home with the kids. Our dinner date ran a little late so, when I got home, I went in to soothe our youngest who was two at the time. I ended up falling asleep with her.

The next morning, I was woken by the cries of the children: "Daddy won't get up!"

I rushed into our bedroom to find him lying on his side on our bed, his eyes half open and a strange liquid oozing from his mouth.

I won't describe the moments of panic that followed. Suffice to say, by the end of the day, we knew that he had had a stroke, and that he was in a coma, with significant damage to his brain. The doctors didn't have much hope.

He was gone, they said, in all but body.

I still cry when I think of the moment I had to call his mother and tell her that her youngest son was in a coma. That was definitely one of the worst moments of my life, one of the most heartbreaking.

Over the next two weeks, we nursed him day and night. His condition hardly changed although I sat with him every day, talking to him, reading Qur'an, making du'a over him. And the people, the people came flooding in during visiting hours. So much love, so much concern, so much support poured forth, both online and in real life. I made du'a for every single person who took the time to make du'a for us, who visited us in the hospital, who cooked food, who was there for us.

One sister, a dear friend, took my children home to her house so that they could continue with their homeschool programme. Another sister (who I hardly knew) gave us the use of her flat for the first week so that I could be close to the hospital. Brothers and sisters, family members, colleagues and employees travelled across Cairo, flew in from abroad, to be there for us, to greet him, to thank him, to find out if we needed anything. It was an outpouring of community support that I will always be grateful for.

As I wrote at the time...

*The words are like water:*
*At times*
*They flow effortlessly*
*Slipping over stones in a stream.*
*At other times*
*They trickle,*
*Painstaking,*
*Drop by drop by drop*
*Until the flow resumes,*
*Because then*
*The words are a waterfall*
*Gushing forth*
*A wall of wonder*
*At one with the world*
*At one with the Word*
*At one with the tears*
*That gush forth*
*Like waterfalls*
*To wash away my worries*
*To wean me off the pain*
*To purify*
*To clarify*
*To cleanse me once again.*
*Word after blessed word*
*Until minutes turn to hours*
*And my hand is damp in yours.*

*Baqarah for protection,*
*Kahf because it's Friday*
*And it's been two weeks*
*And I miss you.*

Two weeks in, I had returned home and was asleep on my boys' bunk bed because I still couldn't bear to go into my own bedroom to sleep in our bed.

The call woke me before Fajr. My heart stopped as I tried to recognize the number on the screen. I drew a blank. But when I answered the phone and heard the familiar voice of the doctor on the other side, I prepared myself for the worst.

And the worst came: my dear husband's heart had stopped beating. They had attempted CPR for thirty minutes with no success.

"JazakAllahu khairan," I whispered hoarsely before cutting off the call. Then I immediately rose from the bed and fell into sujood of shukr. Alhamdulillah.

It was the moment I had been dreading but also the moment I had been preparing myself for, ever since a sister, who had come to visit me at the hospital, had told me the story of a husband and wife whose daughter was desperately ill. Every time they came to the hospital, the doctors would tell them more reasons why she was not going to make it. And, at every visit, the father would turn to his wife and say, "Don't forget".

This continued for several days, the doctors predicting the worst, and the husband reminding his wife not to forget, until the day they arrived and were given the news that would break any parent's heart: their daughter had died.

Upon hearing the news, the husband turned to his wife and said to her, "Now," and they both fell into sujood of shukr.

The hospital staff were amazed, some of them horrified. Surely this was a terribly sad event, one to be wept over, to be mourned, not to be celebrated with sujood?

They asked the couple why, why had they done this?

And the couple told the staff at that hospital how they had taken the decision to give thanks for their daughter's life, for the joy she had brought them, for the love they had shared with her. Allah (swt) had allowed them to love and care for her for all those years: should they not give thanks for this?

And, when I heard this story, I decided that that was what I was going to do, if it ever came to that.

And so that is what I did.

But when your husband of fifteen years, the father of your five children, your protector, your confidante and best friend suddenly is no more, I cannot tell you how profound the sense of loss is. Your entire world is tilted on its axis, everything shifts, and nothing is as it was. You question your place in the world, your identity, your responsibilities, the future. And, for a time, you wander, lost, in that hazy time of mourning, the *'iddah*, seeking out the meaning, the purpose of this test.

What does Allah (swt) want from me?
Why did He choose this test for me?
What am I supposed to do now?

You see, sometimes, the test may come as a short, sharp shock. You are stunned, then you process, then you accept and get ready to move on; to deal with your new reality.

But after that initial shock, there are more tests to come. Tests that come like waves, starting small, bearable, building into ever greater swells of uncertainty and fear. The tests keep coming, stretching their fingers into your days and nights; following you for the weeks and months to come. You have no idea when they will end, when they will release their grip. And you realise that you were ready for the sharpness of loss at the first bite, but not so well prepared for the ongoing trial. That is what it is like when you lose a spouse.

There is a delicate tension in the state of *'iddah*, the mourning period for a widow.

On the one hand, life continues, particularly if you have children or have to work to support your family. The pressures, demands and responsibilities are real and they won't wait for four months and ten days to be over. In this space, you are forced to plan, to look forward, to move on, to face the world. It can be an exquisite distraction from the pain that lies buried deep under the school run, bedtime stories and endless paperwork and deadlines.

On the other hand, your state of *'iddah* restricts you; you cannot fully embrace life, even if you feel ready to. You must pause. You must reflect. You must withdraw. You must face the reality, brave the darkness: the pain, the loneliness, the anger, the fear, the feeling of being bereft. You must face it because it will break you down, bring you to your knees, make you feel once again that vulnerability of his last days when you would have given anything for one last apology, one last kiss, one last promise. You must face the reality that this is Allah's plan for you. And that, if this is so, there must be khair in it for you. It's there. It's there in the chance to ask for forgiveness, to pour your heart out, to cleanse, to rectify your soul, to purify your habits, to be ready to emerge from your *'iddah* like a butterfly from a chrysalis: reborn, refashioned, beautiful.

Of course, I cried. I lost weight. I lost sleep. But, for some reason, a mercy perhaps, I didn't lose sight of the fact that I was still here. I was still standing. And that, somehow, there was a reason for that. A Divine reason. People often ask me how I was able to come back from that challenge, recover from that setback, and keep doing what I do. And I realise that the explanation is this:

**My life path is my own. Allah (swt) has created me unique, with my own set of gifts and talents, challenges and trials, and there is a reason I am still here.**

**I still have work to do.**
**I still have something to contribute.**
**I still have a legacy to build.**
**I am needed here.**

But the only way I can do the work, make my contribution and build my legacy is if I 'Show Up'. Show up as myself, authentic, vulnerable, trusting in Allah (swt) and trusting in the process.

So many of us who have experienced a loss or a setback allow that test to define us: we become 'widows', 'divorcees', 'single parents', 'unemployed', 'childless' and we start to live a life that is tied to our identity as victims, as martyrs.

And, if there is no other message that you take from this book, let it be this one: *you get to choose how to tell your life story*. Every individual is in one of three states: they have either been tested, they are being tested or they are going to be tested. This is the way of the world and it is the sunnah of Allah (swt).

So, now that you know that tests are inevitable, you have a choice: to wear the label of a victim and allow your tests to define you, or reframe your story as a hero's quest.

Remember, the hero of the story never has an easy ride. She meets challenge after challenge on her way to self-awareness, personal growth and a satisfying ending. With every challenge, she grows stronger. With every test, she becomes more faithful. With every loss, she gains in wisdom, clarity and depth. So that, by the end of her life story, she is a better version of herself: forged in the fires of life's ups and downs, she emerges a diamond.

So, how do we become the heroes of our life story?

We must *recognise* that this life is the one chance we have to live our purpose, to make a difference, to leave a legacy. We must make a choice to 'Show Up'.

Show up for the sake of Allah (swt).
Show up for your family.
Show up for your circle.
Show up for your community.
Show up for yourself.

# Why now?

There are three reasons why I am writing this to you today, urging you to show up.

●● Because you were created for a noble, lofty purpose, with unique capabilities and potential: so wasting your life hiding behind a mask of excuses and fears just won't cut it;

●● Because you don't know how long you have on this earth: so putting off being present and showing up for yourself and those around you until 'someday' is not a viable option;

●● You only get one chance to show up: most people won't ever experience the sense of satisfaction and fulfilment that comes with showing up fully, sincerely and authentically, before they leave this world – don't be one of this unfortunate majority!

# NOTES

# 2

# WHAT is 'Showing Up'?

Sometimes, it can be easier to define something by describing its opposite and the opposite of showing up is multi-faceted and complex:

- It is pretending to be someone you're not.
- It is not being fully present or mindful with your loved ones.
- It is performing your roles in life with a sense of resentment or martyrdom.
- It is playing the role of 'victim'.
- It is wearing a mask.
- And above all, it is hiding your true self.

There are so many reasons why we hide. We fear the judgement of others, we fear not measuring up. We fear criticism and condemnation. And, most of all, we fear failure.

The fear stops us from being ourselves and from facing life with optimism and courage.

Showing up is so different: to show up is to be present, mind and body, to take responsibility, to take ownership. To bring your true self to whatever role you are called on to play, with all your imperfections and vulnerability in tow. It is to recommit to your life and your purpose. It is to perform the role you were created to fulfil, to do the work you were put here to do. I define 'Showing Up' as an action and an attitude.

**It is to become the hero of your life story.**

So many of us will live mediocre lives, struggling to find our sense of purpose, struggling to achieve anything significant, struggling to make any sort of impact. A major reason for this is that the average person prefers ease to hard work, prefers to make excuses, rather than take responsibility, and prefers to play the victim rather than assume the mantle of the hero.

Most of us find it easier to sleepwalk through life, with a vague feeling that there should be more to life than this, but without the motivation or determination to find out just how much more there is. Or, we convince ourselves that 'someday', we will change, we will step up, we will do things differently. Unfortunately, however, 'someday' is merely a figment of our imagination. It is a fictional time in an unknown future and saying, "I will do such-and-such someday", is tantamount to saying, "I know I should/could do such-and-such, but I can't be bothered".

You can't be bothered?

But this is your life! The one and only life you have on this earth, to make a success of it, or to mess it up: the choice is yours. Every hour that you waste, every day that you allow to slip away, every week that you live unintentionally, every month that you sleepwalk through, adds up to your existence, the sum total of your time here. What do you want your time here to amount to? What story do you want to be able to tell at the end of your days? What legacy will you leave behind?

I am not saying any of this to guilt trip you. I know the lure of lethargy and the power of procrastination; I get it. I just won't accept it, not for me and not for you. If you don't make a change now, next week will look the same as this week. And next year will look the same as this year.

So, my dear sister, understand this:

**If you don't make a decision to show up, and show up now, you may never do it. Because, let's face it, it's easier not to, right? Especially when most people around us are living life on autopilot, sleepwalking through their days.**

What do I mean by 'sleepwalking'? This is when we live out our days stuck in a seemingly endless routine, going through the motions, with no clear goals or ambitions to aim higher or achieve better or experience more. And this could be in any and every area of our lives: spiritually, emotionally, intellectually, socially, professionally. You name it, there are people sleepwalking through it.

But the cost of sleepwalking is high, so very high. Whenever I think of the millions of us who are living our lives on autopilot,

I think of waste: wasted potential, wasted opportunities, wasted lives.

How many of us will live out our days in a state of numbness and detachment, never fully engaging in the activities and relationships around us, keeping up a facade that tells the world that we are fine, that everything is alright, while we are dying inside? How many of us will continue to serve those who need us, sacrificing and putting others first, while our own hopes and dreams wither away inside us, forever unspoken, forever unlived. How many of us will let ourselves go, physically, mentally, emotionally, spiritually, because it's just too hard to pull ourselves back from the brink?

Yes, I know that Allah's Qadr determines our fate. We should not ask "what if?" But I ask you this:

**Do you know what Allah (swt) has written for you? Have you been shown your future? Do you have any reason to believe that Allah has decreed a life of mediocrity and frustration for you? Do you have any reason *not* to believe that He has decreed abundance, happiness and contentment for you? Do you?**

So many of us settle for less and use the excuse of Qadr: "This is what Allah (swt) has decreed for me." But know this: very often, we use this expression as an excuse for inaction. As a way to mask the fact that we can't be bothered. That we would rather sleepwalk than wake up and face the fact that there are some changes that need to be made, that there is work to be done, that we have it in us to do better, to be better.

You are better than using Qadr as an excuse for your lack of satisfaction with your life. If you want more out of life, you have to make more effort. Because life is funny like that – you get out what you put in.

**"Allah (swt) tells us that He will not change the condition of a people until they change what is within themselves."**
**(Qur'an 13:11)**

It really makes you think, doesn't it?

If we want to see change, if we want to see progress, if we want things to get better, *we* have to make moves. *We* have to take action. Then anticipate Allah's mercy with faith, hope and optimism.

As Hal Elrod says in his fantastic little book, *The Miracle Morning*, 'You have to *be* the person you need to be and *do* the things you need to do in order to *have* the things you want to have'.

So, if we want a life that feels satisfying, fulfilling, purposeful and worth getting excited about, we have to *be* different and we have to *do* things differently from the vast majority of people.

If you want more faith, more barakah, more love, more laughter, more meaningful moments, more beautiful memories, confidence, resilience and a sense of purpose, you'll need to make some changes to the way you think, to the way you respond to challenges, to the way you walk in the world.

It may feel uncomfortable at times. It may feel like you are swimming against the tide. More than once, you will feel like giving up.

But remember this:

**Your decision to start showing up is the beginning of a journey, a beautiful journey towards both self-acceptance and fulfilling your highest potential. Isn't that worth a bit of discomfort?**

**Now is the time for it, if not now, then when? And, if not you, then who?**

From this day forth, refuse to settle for mediocrity and make a decision, right now, to start stepping up, to start leveling up and to start showing up.

## Showing up: A Prophetic Sunnah

If we define 'Showing Up' as stepping up to take on one's role in life – of accepting responsibility for our actions and responses, of being ourselves, even in our imperfections – we will find plenty of examples in our Islamic history.

The books of Sirah are full of stories of men, women and children who showed up, despite the odds, and went on to fully live their purpose. There is gold in so many of their stories but I will share only that of the Last Messenger, Prophet Muhammad (pbuh).

One of the things I love about the life story of the Prophet (pbuh) is how *inspiring* it is. So many of the tests he endured would have sent a lesser man into victim mode – with good reason!

Take a look at some of the more difficult aspects of his life: being an orphan; marrying an older woman who had been divorced and widowed; reviled and persecuted for his beliefs; being cast out of his city and exiled; witnessing multiple deaths in his family, including his own children; leaving behind no sons to carry his name; impoverished; and carrying the responsibility for an entire nation on his shoulders.

But the Prophet Muhammad's life is a beautiful illustration of showing up: following your heart, doing the right thing – even if you have to bear the consequences – pushing through fear and doubt, showing love and kindness openly, in a culture that denigrated such traits, embracing humility, even in victory.

In spite of the odds, our Messenger (pbuh) showed up and became the hero of, not just his own life story, but the history of the Muslims. We would not be who we are today, we would not believe what we believe today, we would not know what we know today, if he hadn't embraced his journey and shown up, ready to do what needed to be done.

I would also like to share with you the story of a woman who was not connected to the Prophet's family, was not a woman of influence or power, was not an influencer, but whose story of bravery and authenticity – her 'showing up story' – has been preserved and has become a part of the Islamic canon of narrations.

This is the story of the daughter who was helping her mother prepare the milk for the next day's market. Wanting to see a greater return on investment for their milk that day, the mother suggested that the girl add water to the milk, in order to make it stretch further. The girl refused, reminding her mother that the caliph at the time, 'Umar ibn Al Khattab, had expressly forbidden this practice.

The mother rebuked her daughter, saying, "Where is the Amir now? He cannot see you!"

To which the daughter replied: "Even if he doesn't see us, surely Allah (swt) sees us."

Why I retell this story as an example of showing up is this:

**Whether we choose to show up in a way that affects generations after us, or simply the one person sitting in the room with us, it matters.**

**It makes a difference. It counts.**

# NOTES

# NOTES

# 3

# What does 'Showing Up' in YOUR life look like?

Every day, you play a multitude of roles:

*Worshipper*
*Woman*
*Wife*
*Mother*
*Daughter*
*Friend*
*Boss*
*Leader*

What would it look like if you showed up – sincerely and authentically – in any one of those roles? How transformational would that be for you and for those who love you?

*If you brought humility to your acts of worship;*
*If you brought joy to your womanhood;*
*If you brought sincerity to your wifely duties;*
*If you brought intention to your mothering;*
*If you brought passion to your work;*
*If you brought focus to your relationships.*

*We don't have to live on autopilot.*
*We can show up as the hero in any given role.*

We can all take the easy route and choose to hide our true selves, rather than stepping into our power and claiming our authentic identity, both for ourselves and others.

I know that I hid behind a particular identity for years. I wanted to be liked and respected by everyone. I wanted to be the acceptable role model. I wanted to live up to everyone's expectations of me.

**But if living up to other people's expectations forces you to hide who you truly are and what you truly believe in, it can be a source of frustration and, more seriously, dissonance.**

For a long time, it was like there were two versions of me: the public version and the private version. And the two were not always aligned. I found myself slipping into one or the other, depending on who I was with, and what was expected of me.

This meant that, while I was showing up in a particular way in public, this wasn't reflected in my private life.

In public, I was a woman of goals and ambitions, a woman who inspired others to level up and aim higher. But, to my own family, I was none of those things. It pains me to say this but, for the longest time, I had been telling myself a story. The story was that I am not a good mother, that being a mum is 'not my thing', that my children don't really need me, that they are not my biggest legacy.

I know that may sound shocking especially as, in Islam, we are encouraged to revere the mother and the role she plays in the stability of the family and raising the next generation.

But that's where I was.

It was a story that helped me to hide from my own failings and weaknesses and made me feel better about the fact that I didn't really have a vision for my family. But it was also a story that was stopping me from getting out of my comfort zone and truly pushing past my fears and self-doubt to find the gold on the other side.

Because, when I decided to challenge that story, and choose a different, more empowering belief – that my children deserve the best of me and they are my greatest gift to the world – everything changed.

I decided to take extreme ownership for my children's development and wellbeing. I decided to stop hiding away behind my work and business, and step out into a new space of vulnerable and authentic leadership. It is scary and unfamiliar, but I can see the benefits already, and so can my children. I am showing up for them, 100% authentic and real. And I know we will all be the better for it, insha Allah.

So, what will showing up look like for you?

Well, as you can imagine, showing up in the different roles you play will look different at different stages of your life. The defining features of showing up, however, do not change:

**Showing up requires you to be present, authentic and sincere.**

Let's have a look at how you could be present, authentic and sincere in the different spheres of your life.

## Showing up for yourself

There are two vital components of showing up for yourself: self-acceptance and self-love. Without these two ingredients, it is far too easy to sleepwalk through your own life, neglecting yourself and your needs and never fully living up to your potential as a blessed creation of Allah (swt).

So, when you think of showing up for yourself, consider these questions:

➥ Am I showing up for myself spiritually? Am I striving to grow closer to Allah (swt), to increase in knowledge and to share what I have learned with others? Am I striving to improve my character, the quality of my *ibadah*, my level of understanding? Am I striving to conquer my nafs and live according to my highest ideals? Or am I coasting, taking my *iman* for granted, making excuses?

◦◦ Am I showing up for myself emotionally? Am I tuning in to my emotions and ensuring that I acknowledge them and deal with them? Am I addressing emotional issues as they arise? Am I working to heal any wounds from my past? Am I communicating my feelings with those around me? Am I taking myself to account and working to develop emotional resilience and fortitude? Or am I ignoring my mental state and suppressing my feelings?

◦◦ Am I showing up for myself physically? Am I taking care of the body that Allah (swt) blessed me with? Am I paying attention to my health and wellbeing? Am I eating healthfully and being active? Or am I neglecting myself, letting myself go or, worse, punishing myself by holding on to habits that I know are not serving me?

◦◦ Am I showing up for myself intellectually? Am I actively learning more about the world around me, improving my understanding and gaining new skills? Am I challenging myself with intellectually stimulating books, talks, workshops, and conversations? Am I pushing myself to discover more about what my mind is capable of mastering? Or am I being lazy, wallowing in complacency, content to stay in the same place intellectually?

# Showing up for your relationship

What does it mean to 'Show Up' as a spouse?

Again, the call to being present and mindful, to being sincere and authentic and bringing your true self to the relationship. This can be difficult for some of us, particularly if we have been taught there is only one way to be a good wife OR if we have been hurt before. In either scenario, it is often easier to simply play the role of the good wife, to do the duties, to say the right things and protect ourselves from being vulnerable and, potentially, getting hurt.

This way, we are safe from judgement and criticism.

But are we truly loving and supporting from an authentic place, as our true selves?

Do we dare to do that?

> *"Your wives are a garment for you, and you are a*
> *garment for them."*
> **(Qur'an 2:187)**

Often, when this verse is mentioned, we are reminded that garments protect and beautify, making us feel loved, secure and safe. Showing up as a wife means doing all this from a place of sincerity and authenticity, from a place of contentment and gratitude.

When we show up as wives who are garments, we strive to adapt, to change. To grow to accommodate our spouse as he grows, or to come in a little, when he needs a little extra support.

As garments, there are times when we will need to lighten, as summer nears, and to grow heavier, when winter beckons.

There are times when we will be simple and homely, and times when we will be utterly gorgeous, depending on the situation, depending on the mood.

In this way, we can achieve synergy with our spouse. To be his positive when he hits a negative. To be his left brain when he is stuck in his right brain mode. To be his pillar when he needs to lean. To be his pillow when he needs to lay. And he can learn to do the same as we allow ourselves to be vulnerable and be reassured by him, to be weak and be strengthened by him, to be in need and receive from him, to fall and be helped up by him.

Showing up in your marriage means bringing your true self to the relationship and being an active and mindful participant in the building of your lives together.

## Showing up for your children

Motherhood can often seem like a blur of never-ending routines, responsibilities and tasks. Demands on our time, attention and energy can leave us feeling drained and lacklustre, causing us to sleepwalk through our days, frustrated and mildly resentful. We go through the motions but, in reality, we have checked out. There is no joy left, no excitement or anticipation, and our children feel it. They can see that Mummy is not happy, that she would rather spend time on her phone than with them, that she is distracted at bedtime and doesn't look into their eyes when they speak to her.

Now I am not here to guilt-trip you into showing up for your children but I will say this: by not showing up as a mother, you run the risk of losing out on the rewards (in both dunyah and akhirah) of being a parent in the first place.

Showing up for your children involves being intentional. It involves being mindful. And it involves being present, in body and, most importantly, in mind. It involves us having a vision for ourselves as mothers and actively working towards that vision. It involves us taking stock, taking ourselves to account, evaluating our behaviour, our attitudes, our reactions and seeking to improve.

It involves seeing our mothering as a work in progress, not a done deal.

## Showing up for your family

The same goes for our role in our families: are we being intentional in our relationships? Are we taking ownership of our responsibilities and executing them with conviction and intention? Are we paying attention to the way we treat our family – and the way our family treats us? Or are we simply going through the motions, doing the bare minimum and hiding our true selves?

## Showing up for your dreams

How many of us have dreams that we have given up on? Plans that we let fall by the wayside? Goals that we allowed to slip away?

I know so many sisters who have had all sorts of dreams: memorising the Qur'an, homeschooling their children, starting a business, travelling, writing a book, becoming financially independent, establishing a charity, adopting, the list is endless...

But it's not easy to hold on to a vision when your circumstances – and the people around you – seem to be telling you that it isn't realistic, that it's impossible.

In the first place, showing up for your dreams means acknowledging their validity.

Showing up for your dreams means considering them valuable and worthy of your time and effort. Showing up for your dreams means honouring your potential to do better, to achieve more, to rise higher, which, of course, comes back to the same thing: honouring yourself.

So make your intention, right now, to start showing up for your dreams and take the necessary action to make them come true.

REFLECTION: What dreams are you harbouring, deep inside? What hopes do you have for the future? What plans do you wish you had the courage to put into action?

## The Circle of Influence

You may be wondering why you making the decision to show up in your life matters, to me or anyone else. You are probably thinking, 'I'm just a mum' or 'I'm nobody famous'. And so I share this story with you and ask you to contemplate the answer to this question: who is in your circle of influence?

Popular American speaker, Sr Zohra Sarwari and I once did a speaking tour of the UK together. During one of the twenty-seven events, we were being hosted by a small mosque in East London. The atmosphere in the room was warm and positive: we had been listening to inspirational and uplifting talks about how we could be proud and brave as Muslim women, how to stand up for our identity and make our mark on society. Many examples of famous Muslim women from the past and present were shared and we were left in no doubt: you can and should make a contribution as a Muslimah.

The floor was opened for questions and a sister put up her hand. "What if you're not famous," she said, her voice edged with hesitation. "What if you don't have a huge Facebook following? What if you're just an ordinary sister?" Her question seemed to resonate with many in the room and the atmosphere became pensive, thoughtful.

Indeed, how *can* we make a difference if we don't have 30K followers on Instagram or Facebook? How can we make an impact if we don't write for a national newspaper? How can we make a change if we are not 'famous'?

I'm here to tell you this:

## We are all influencers, every one of us.

This is because we all have a 'circle of influence', a group of people who love us, trust us and look to us for guidance.

Think about it: is it your children or your immediate family? Is it your halaqah group or the girls at college? Is it your work colleagues or your employees? Is it the children in your classroom or the members of the board? Is it your local masjid or community centre? Is it your Facebook account or a

Whatsapp group you're on? Is it your blog, website, Twitter or those 30k followers on Instagram?

Now, do you see how the circle is widening?

We have all been blessed with certain characteristics, certain traits, that make us perfect to fulfil the mission we have on this earth: to worship Allah (swt) with every fibre of our being, in a myriad of different ways. Part of worshipping Allah is being a bringer of khair, of good, into the lives of others. There are no numbers here, no tally charts: there is only quality.

**If you strive to make a difference to the lives of the people in your circle of influence, and trust Allah (swt) to do the rest, you are on your way to showing up and making a lasting contribution, one that will be remembered long after you are gone, bi'idhnillah.**

# NOTES

# 4

# The HOW of 'Showing Up'

Now that you know that you are an influencer in your everyday life, let's address the elephant in the room. Sometimes, you just don't feel like showing up because, quite frankly, it is easier to go through each day on autopilot.

You wake up at the same time every day, to the sound of the same alarm. You pray, maybe read some Qur'an if you're at that level, or simply stumble on into the maelstrom of morning routines: waking children up, rooting through piles of clean clothes to find uniforms, making lunches, hurtling into the traffic of the school run, waving them off, perhaps heaving a sigh of relief. Then back to the house or on to the office: to complete tasks, tick boxes, dot i's and cross t's. Then it's back to the house, to the children, to the needs of the family: cooking dinner, checking homework, baths, bedtime, collapse.

And every day, on repeat.

Not to mention the pressure you feel coming in from all sides: from family, friends, social media, TV, government. Pressure to think a certain way, act a certain way, look a certain way, behave a certain way.

It's exhausting.

Sometimes, the responsibilities, and expectations, and disappointments, can feel like an onslaught. And, sometimes, the only way to respond is to go numb. The numbness takes away the pain.

I remember clearly when I realised that I was numbing myself to get through each day. From the outside looking in, I had it all under control but, on the inside, my world was falling apart. It was soon after I had remarried and moved back to the UK with my children. I had stopped taking care of myself and had gained weight. I couldn't get a comb through my hair nor could I remember the last time I wore something nice. I looked in the mirror and I saw the grey hairs, the bags under my eyes, the lines.

Something inside me screamed: No! This is not you. You are better than this. Take back control. Do something!

But the effort was too much. I allowed the numbness to take over and sedate me.

I had also stopped reading my girls their bedtime stories. Once upon a time, it was a ritual that bonded us and provided a transition from waking to sleeping. The hallmark of a happy childhood. But I had become so rushed off my feet, so tired at the end of the day, so stretched, that the five minutes it took to read a book was too much effort.

Something inside me cried out: No! Don't waste these years. They will be gone before you know it. Treasure them while you still can. Make the time!

But the effort was too much. I allowed the numbness to take over and convince me that this was my new normal.

I had stopped sharing my thoughts and dreams with my new husband and I felt further away from him than ever. I used to read books on how to have a healthy marriage and eagerly apply all the experts' advice. I was always the one to come up with ideas for date night, to leave a thoughtful note, or plan an exciting getaway for two. But I could feel myself shutting down, becoming sullen and every "I love you" felt like a lie.

Something inside me pleaded: No! Don't take him for granted. You don't know how long you have. Love is a verb. Love like you mean it!

But the effort was too much. I allowed the numbness to take over and persuade me that I didn't care anyway.

In that phase, when I had allowed myself to grow numb, I ceased to feel the disappointment in myself for the million and one things I knew I could be doing better.

I called it acceptance, but, in reality, I had taken the easy way out: I had given up. And the numbness, the giving up, is the antithesis of showing up.

When we allow ourselves to go numb and start to sleepwalk through our lives, we think we are protecting ourselves but, in reality, we are missing out on living a rich, meaningful and purpose-filled life.

We are missing out on living an intentional life.

**"We cannot selectively numb emotions, when we numb the painful emotions, we also numb the positive emotions." Brené Brown**

## *Open*

*I am open to this journey*
*I am open to this quest*
*I am open to this moment*
*I am open to this test.*
*I accept*
*I flow*
*I submit*
*I grow*
*I go forth*
*I know*
*That He is with me*
*Every step of the way*
*And that He will catch me*
*At the end of the day.*
*He always has*
*And He always will.*

So, what steps can we take towards showing up more authentically in our lives?

Well, I have distilled my roadmap into six steps that, if followed, will lead you to a more present, productive, powerful version of yourself, bi'idhnillah.

Are you ready?
Let's do this.

# STEP ONE: BE INTENTIONAL

As Muslims, we know the importance of intentions. Intentions can transform a seemingly mundane act into a lofty act of worship and, by the same token, a lack of intention can leave a seemingly noble deed devoid of barakah.

The Prophet (pbuh) taught us that actions are but by intention and that every one of us will only be rewarded according to our intention.

'Umar Ibn Al-Khattab relates that he heard the Messenger of Allah (pbuh) say, *"Verily actions are by intentions, and for every person is what he intended. So the one whose hijrah was to Allah and His Messenger, then his hijrah was to Allah and His Messenger. And the one whose hijrah was for the world to gain from it, or a woman to marry her, then his hijrah was to what he made hijrah for."* (Bukhari & Muslim)

He also taught us that a pure intention is a prerequisite for our deeds being accepted by Allah (swt). And that is why being intentional, mindful of why we are doing what we do, is so important.

But what does it actually mean to 'set your intention' for a particular action? It means to get clear on the true value, the deeper meaning of that act. When evaluating the activities you do on a daily basis, it might be useful to consider the following questions:

> •❖ What is that act worth with Allah (swt)?
>
> •❖ What does that act – and your ability to perform it – mean to you on a deeper level?
>
> •❖ What does that act communicate to those whom you serve? What does it say to them about you?

I think a perfect example of this is the simple act of cooking for the family. It is so easy to do this mindlessly, without a sense of purpose or intention. It's just something that has to be done, right? It's even possible to resent it or consider it a burdensome chore or even a waste of time. I know I have felt this way before and, every time I find myself slipping into autopilot, I ask myself those questions.

*What is this act worth with Allah (swt)?*

*What does this act – and my ability to perform it – mean to me on a deeper level?*

*What does this act communicate to those whom I serve? What does it say to them about me?*

And, more often than not, I am able to reconnect with the higher purpose of these meals I prepare; what a blessing it is to be able to cook for my family, what my showing up to lovingly prepare these meals – day in, day out – says to my family about what they all mean to me.

Personally, I have found that reflecting in this way on the acts of service that I regularly perform changes my attitude towards them. It changes my attitude towards my family and towards my life in general. All of a sudden, I am able to appreciate the great blessing there is in serving my family in this way, and how it makes my family feel cared for and loved.

> REFLECTION: What other areas of your life could benefit from this more intentional approach? Look, in particular, at acts of service or contribution that you do as a normal part of your routine. Find the gems there: those acts that can perform 'double duty': good in this life and in the next.

So many of us suffer, not from a lack of purpose or meaning in our lives, but an inability to recognise that purpose, that meaning. We compare ourselves constantly. We judge ourselves because we are not as 'active' as that sister, or as 'knowledgeable' as the other sister. We are so hard on ourselves that we end up paralysed by low self-esteem and self-doubt.

But here's the thing:

**There is no need to beat ourselves up because we
are not like this sister, that sister and the next sister.
We simply need to be intentional in how we show up
*in our lives*, doing whatever we do sincerely for
Allah (swt) and doing it in the very best way.
Miraculously, the rest will take care of itself.**

# Bloom Where You Are Planted

When my late husband passed away, I remember being acutely aware of the fact that I was (a) one of only a few sisters in the public eye, and (b) one of the only ones who was now a widow. What was the lesson? I wondered. Was there some significance to the fact that I had lost my husband while playing such a public role in our community?

I concluded that there was. Maybe it was a test for me. Maybe there were spiritual and emotional muscles I needed to build. Maybe it was a reminder for the thousands who looked on. Maybe it was all of the above.

Either way, I knew that Allah (swt) had chosen for me to undergo that particular trial at that particular time in my life to get me to show up in a particular way, to step into a new role and meet the challenges head-on.

**I chose to see that challenge, not as a setback but, as a set up for a comeback.**

Think about it: haven't we all been presented with our own challenges, tailored uniquely to us and our situation?

One sister has ageing parents to care for, another sister has several children, or has children with disabilities, or fosters, or volunteers on the school committee. One sister has a demanding job, another sister is setting up her own business, or has been running one for years, or is supporting her children on a single salary. One sister does talks around the world, another sister writes articles, another performs poetry, or paints, or shares her passions with her huge social media following.

All are required to show up differently, in their own unique way, with the gifts that Allah (swt) gave them and the circumstances He put them in. The beauty is in recognising the opportunities for blessings in *your* unique situation.

So, take a few moments to think about your life. Where has Allah (swt) placed you in relation to others? What strengths has He already blessed you with in order to be able to show up fully in that situation? Recognise the good you are already doing and then clarify your intention, renew it so that it elevates even the most mundane act to an act of worship. Then make the intention to show up fully, in an even better way, in a more mindful way, in a way that embodies ihsan, excellence.

## A Crisis of Confidence

I once had a conversation with a sister who shared with me that she never felt comfortable accepting praise from people for the work that she did. Although she was clearly skillful at communicating and sharing her gifts of empathy and compassion with others, she struggled to name her strengths and skills in an exercise she had been asked to do in one of my programmes.

"I don't feel I deserve their praise," she said. "That belongs to Allah (swt)."

Can you relate to that sentiment?

Humility is considered a noble characteristic in Islam. It was a feature of the Prophet's personality and is emphasised in numerous ayahs from the Qur'an and Hadith.

To be humble is, by its strict definition, to have a low estimation of one's importance. In other words, meek, deferential, submissive and self-effacing.

Pride on the other hand, is considered a negative characteristic, being linked to arrogance, haughtiness and Satan himself. Allah (swt) says in the Qur'an, as part of a longer ayah: *"Except Iblees (Satan), he was proud and was one of the disbelievers." (Qur'an 38:74)*

So, on the one hand, we have humility, which erases the self, and, on the other, we have pride, which overvalues the self, leading to disbelief and sin.

Where then does confidence fit in?

Confidence is defined as the feeling or belief that one can have faith in or rely on someone or something. Self-confidence would mean that one can have faith in or rely on oneself, that one can trust in one's abilities, qualities and judgement. Other words to denote self-confidence are assertive, positive, composed, and poised.

And yet, time and again, sisters have expressed to me that they struggle with confidence because they don't want to seem proud or arrogant. However, this inability to embrace confidence has a direct impact on your ability to show up in your life.

So, is there any room in a Muslim's character for confidence? Is a confident Muslim woman, in fact, a contradiction in terms?

Going back to the sister I mentioned at the start, I wanted to share with her a different way of looking at other people's words of praise. Rather than seeing them as assaults to be warded off with a self-effacing "I'm not really that good", why not see them as reminders of Allah's Mercy, His generosity, His gifts to you? Why not use that opportunity to return to Him in praise and gratitude? Why waste that opportunity by denying the truth: that you have been gifted with abilities and skills that are needed and appreciated by others?

If you are fortunate enough to have people around you who thank you for what you bring, who are appreciative of and acknowledge your skills, talents or wonderful qualities, don't squander that. Hear what they are saying. Allow it to sink in. And allow it to make you grateful to Allah (swt), the Giver of all these gifts. Because the fact is this:

**Allah (swt) has blessed us all with unique gifts, talents and abilities. This is an indisputable fact.**

So who does it serve when you deny those gifts?
Who does it serve when you efface those talents?
Who does it serve when you denigrate those abilities?

Who cares if you 'can't take compliments'? Just say 'Alhamdulillah!' and keep doing your thing!

After all, Allah (swt) has blessed you, many, many times over. Should that not make you grateful?

Allah (swt) has made you promises. Should that not make you poised?

Allah (swt) has control over all things and is your Protecting Friend. Should that not make you confident?

If there *is* a tension between being confident and having humility, denigrating yourself or denying Allah's gifts is not the way to resolve it.

**Acknowledge your gifts, celebrate your abilities, be grateful for your talents. Because this opens up a whole new world of abundance for you: a world in which you can explore your strengths, work on developing your skills, build your confidence so that you can truly show up for those who love and trust you.**
**Your circle of influence.**

# I am not worthy

As we demonstrated earlier, every one of us has a circle of influence and yet we waste the opportunity to lead because we tell ourselves a particular story: a story that we are unworthy, that we are not good enough, that we will never measure up.

**I'm here to tell you that you are worthy, that you are good enough and that all you need to measure up to, is your best self.**

*"Allah does not burden a soul with more than it can bear..."* (Qur'an 2:286)

You are worthy of the role that Allah (swt) has assigned to you: as a leader, as a supporter, as a defender, as a cheerleader. Allah (swt) knows you intimately – strengths, weaknesses – the whole package. And He has placed you on this earth to fulfil certain roles – you know what they are. Trust that He knows what He is doing. You are here, in this time and in this place, for a reason. There is something your people need that only you can give. Acknowledge that. Accept that. Allow it to seep into your subconscious. Allow it to fill you with a sense of honour and purpose. Allah (swt) has *entrusted* you with this flock. And, as long as you show up, authentically and sincerely, He will help you. You aren't expected to do it all on your own: you put in the work, He brings the results. Simple and oh so reassuring.

**You are good enough for His blessings; acknowledge and appreciate the gifts and He will bless you with even more.**

## STEP TWO: BE POSITIVE

**"Whether you think you can or you think you can't, you're right." Henry Ford**

Our attitude plays a huge part in how we show up from day to day. It doesn't matter how talented you are, how educated, how well-connected; if you believe that you are not able to do something, the chances of you excelling are slim to none.

Think about it: if you've already decided that a particular feat cannot be accomplished, are you really going to put in the time, effort and sheer hard work that it takes to achieve almost anything? Of course not! You've already decided that it's not going to happen and so, even as you make the right sounds and some half-hearted moves, you've already chosen how this story is going to end. It becomes a self-fulfilling prophecy.

That is why having and maintaining a positive attitude is so important if you are going to show up in your life: it is the fuel to your fire.

The positive attitude, the 'I can do this' vibe, is powerful. It gives you confidence when embarking on whatever mission you have set for yourself and it gives you strength when you encounter setbacks, too. If you've already decided that you are going to make it, that you've got this, that you're going to push through, even when the going gets tough, chances are, you'll do just that.

So how do we cultivate a positive attitude?

Firstly, remember that our deen encourages us to be optimistic, to think well of Allah (swt) and to trust that He wants the very best for us.

The Prophet (pbuh) said, "*Allah the Most High said, 'I am as My servant thinks (expects) I am. I am with him when he mentions Me. If he mentions Me to himself, I mention him to Myself; and if he mentions Me in an assembly, I mention him in an assembly greater than it. If he draws near to Me a hand's length, I draw near to him an arm's length. And if he comes to Me walking, I go to him at speed.'*" (Bukhari)

"*I am as my servant thinks I am.*"

Let us just ponder on this sentence for a minute.

If you choose to believe that Allah (swt) is punishing you, wants you to suffer, and is withholding His blessings, don't be surprised if you find your life full of suffering, trials and disappointment.

If, on the other hand, you choose to believe that Allah (swt) is Kind and that He has blessed you with abundance and that His plans are always in your favour, don't be surprised to find your life full of gratitude and joy and abundance.

It's all available.

How else would you explain those people who are tested and tried with all manner of things – poverty, hardship, illness, loss – and are still smiling, are still grateful, are still finding the joy in every day? It has nothing to do with their circumstances; it is all about the decision they made to focus on what they have, rather than what they don't have.

Conversely, how about those who, from the outside, have everything – health, security, love, prestige – and yet find themselves drowning in negativity, depression and suicidal thoughts? Again, the circumstances don't matter; it is the mindset that makes the difference.

**Expecting good from Allah is a powerful mindset tool that He has given us. Use it.**

> REFLECTION: Ask yourself, what do you hope for from your Lord? Do you believe that you are abundant and that He is more than capable of giving you all that you dreamed of and more? Or do you feel shy to ask Allah (swt) for the things that you crave, the big things that seem almost too big? Do you think asking for more makes you ungrateful?

Once again, the importance and power of a positive attitude becomes clear when we remember that Allah (swt) tells us in the Qur'an: *"If you are grateful, I will surely increase you (in favour)."* (Qur'an 14:7)

And the essence of gratitude is positivity: an overriding optimism about your life in all its complexity and wonder. The ability to recognise and acknowledge your blessings is a crucial component of both positivity and gratitude: they're twin sisters!

So, as you strive to show up in your life, it is crucial to cultivate a positive outlook:

**You are here for a reason, blessed to be here, in this time, in this place, doing the work that Allah (swt) wants you to do, making a difference in your own unique way: own that! And allow a positive, grateful optimism to light your way.**

## How you tell your story

I'd like to begin by telling you the story of two women who lived long ago.

The first woman was born to a noble family and enjoyed a privileged upbringing. She married well, but that marriage ended in widowhood. She married again, and that marriage ended in divorce. This meant that she was now a woman who had been married multiple times; divorced and widowed.

When she married again, she married a man much younger than her, a man without a noble name or wealth. And that man soon became an object of hostility and ridicule, causing her to lose her status and all the comforts she was used to as her community boycotted them and made life unbearable. And then that woman died, leaving behind that man and their children.

The second woman was also born to a noble family. But she was married off at a young age, to an older man. Not only was he older, but he also had other wives. She lived in poverty for most of her life, often not having more than dates and water, and no worldly possessions to speak of. She endured hardships and slander and, when her husband died, she was left childless, with no sons or daughters to care for her in her old age.

Do you recognise these women?

As you may have guessed, the first woman is our mother, Khadijah bint Kuwaylid (ra) and the second is our mother A'isha bint Abu Bakr (ra).

You may have recognised the women – but did you recognise the descriptions?

Have you ever thought of Khadijah (ra) as a divorcee or widow, worthy of scorn?

Have you ever thought of A'isha (ra) as a barren woman, worthy of ridicule?

We never think of them that way because we don't ever tell their stories with them playing the role of victim. We cast them as the heroines they were.

Yes, Khadijah (ra) was a divorcee and widow but she was also a loyal wife, a successful businesswoman, a pillar of strength for the Prophet (pbuh) and the fledgling Muslim community. That is her legacy.

Yes, A'isha (ra) was married young and widowed childless, but she was also a beloved wife, a brave and generous spirit and a scholar and teacher of Hadith and fiqh. That is her legacy.

All the above are historical facts. It is what we choose to focus on that determines whether we pity them for their hard lives or admire them for their bravery. Both interpretations are available. And this is the case for every single person who has shown up, in spite of the challenges, in spite of the pain.

Think of that single mother who, in spite of the hardships, manages to make her children feel loved and safe.

Think of that sister who has been trying for years to get married, to no avail, but manages to hold on to her faith, in spite of the challenges.

Think of that sister who, after years in an abusive marriage, manages to flee and finds the strength to start again.

Think of the refugee who manages to hold on to hope in spite of having lost her home, her husband and her country.

If we focused on their circumstances, we could easily write them off as victims to be pitied and patronised. But when we shift our focus to how they respond to their circumstances, we are able to see them for the heroic individuals they really are.

## Stories we tell ourselves

There are always at least two sides to any story. As I illustrated in the previous section, even the most tragic of personal stories can be told in two ways: as a victim's story or a hero's tale.

How many times, when you think about your own experiences, particularly the challenging ones, have you focused on the difficulty and pain of the trial, rather than the strength and resilience you showed? How many times have you focused on the wrong actions of others, rather than the dignity and patience you displayed? And how many times have you focused on the short-term challenges of the test, rather than the lessons that it taught you in the long-term?

If you're like most of us, you will have slipped into the victim mode plenty of times, perhaps so often that you have grown to believe the victim narrative. And, sometimes, our peers will encourage us to assume victim status: we are easier to sympathise with when we are pathetic. But the trouble with assuming victim status is that it disempowers you in the long run. The victim narrative tells you that you have no choice, no agency, that everything bad has been *done to* you, that you have no options, that you have no responsibility, that you are powerless.

And when we tell ourselves that we have no choices, no power, guess what? We start to behave that way. We stop fighting the feelings of despair and desperation. We stop resisting the pull of misery and complacency. We stop reaching for the things that will help us get through our pain and confusion: the salah, du'a, and the practical help of others.

It is like a woman who is drowning and, believing that she is destined to die this way, gives up and stops swimming for the surface. Could she have survived if she had kept struggling to reach the light? Possibly. The truth is, we will never know.

Could you survive that divorce with your dignity and self-confidence intact? Possibly. If you don't try, we will never know.

Could you get over the loss of your child with your faith and patience intact? Possibly. If you don't try, we will never know.

Could you accept the loss of your job as an opportunity to do something more meaningful with your life and finally live your dreams? Possibly. If you don't try, we will never know.

Whenever you think of a loss – any loss – think of what was gained in the process. Was it increased *iman*? Appreciation? Clarity? Acceptance? Serenity? Strength? Patience? Gratitude? A fresh outlook? A fresh start?

Allah (swt) tells us, in no uncertain terms, that He will not burden us more than we can bear. And that promise applies to us individually, as well as collectively. Allah (swt) knows our condition better than we know ourselves. And He chooses our tests accordingly.

So know this:

**If He has chosen a particular test for you, you can get through it. There is an opportunity there for you to grow in closeness to Him, in awareness of yourself, in gratitude for all that is good in your life. Don't waste it.**

And never lose sight of the fact that we are permanently in one of three states: we've either been tested, we are being tested or we will be tested.

And so, in the deep darkness of that test – whatever it may be – when you feel helpless, hopeless and alone, and you despair of ever feeling whole again, fix your heart firmly on Allah's promise: *"After difficulty, there is ease. Indeed, after difficulty, there is ease."* (Qur'an 94:5–6)

The clouds *will* part. The dawn *will* come. The ease is promised. Hold on for the dawn.

You get to choose how to tell your life story. Will you cast yourself in the victim role or will you live to tell the tale of the heroine who survived the challenges, who rose after every fall, who came back after every setback, who fought to the end, never losing hope, never losing faith, and lived to tell the tale?

REFLECTION: What story have you been telling about your life? And how could a retelling of your own narrative help you to show up more authentically and sincerely in your life?

# Limiting beliefs

Very often, the story we tell about our life is based on a set of beliefs and values that we have built up over time. We have held these beliefs for so long, and gathered so much evidence to back them up, that we now see them as facts, indisputable facts, set in stone.

> *"I always quit…"*
> *"I'm not clever…"*
> *"I am a bad mother…"*
> *"We will never be happy together…"*
> *"I have no time…"*
> *"I will never accomplish anything…"*

A belief is, by definition, something that we hold to be true. However, when we discuss beliefs in this section, we are not talking about belief in Allah (swt) and the tenets of Islam; we are talking about the beliefs we have about who we are, who we aren't, who we should be and who we shouldn't be.

I first learned about limiting beliefs from my good friend, LaYinka Sanni, a certified NLP Practitioner and coach. She outlines four categories of limiting beliefs:

- Identity
- Cause
- Meaning
- Possibility and judgement

What these categories look like in real life is this, for example: "I am a bad mum." That would be an example of a limiting belief related to your identity.

Limiting beliefs related to cause become apparent when we say things like "I am a bad mum because my mother was distant and never showed me love."

Limiting beliefs can also pop up in the meaning that we give to things: "He is always late because he doesn't care about me."

And lastly, possibly the most pernicious form of limiting belief is this one: "I could never do X", "I should not feel Y", "I must accept X".

> REFLECTION: Can you identify any beliefs you have that fit into the above categories? How have those beliefs been limiting you?

Many of us govern our whole lives by a set of limiting beliefs. I hear it all the time when sisters speak to me about why they have not achieved more in their lives. They are carrying decades of criticism and blame, often from childhood. They have internalised it all and it seeps out in conversation: I hear the self-doubt, I hear the self-sabotage, I hear the barriers and blockages. Most of these can be traced back to limiting beliefs that have become internalised as the story they tell about who they are unfolds.

Now the interesting thing about the brain is that, like most of us, it wants to be right. So, once you have told this story a few times, your brain becomes adept at interpreting events in a way that confirms the story. This, in essence, is confirmation bias. The ability of the brain to interpret new evidence in a way that confirms existing beliefs.

You can imagine how damaging it is if these beliefs are, in fact, limiting beliefs.

If someone believes, for example, that they are a bad mother, confirmation bias dictates that she will interpret everything that happens through the lens of her poor maternal skills. Her son doesn't have an easy time potty training? It's because she is a bad mother. Her daughter struggles to read while her classmates sail through? It's because she is a bad mother. When in this state, it doesn't matter how much evidence there is to the contrary; it is as if the brain merely filters that information out and highlights the events that could be interpreted in a way that confirms the already held beliefs.

This is the same whether the story is about ourselves or about others: our spouse, children, parents, friends, colleagues.

> REFLECTION: It might be helpful to take some time to look into your limiting beliefs about yourself and others and try to spot when confirmation bias is at play. And actively question the assumptions you are making about yourself and others, particularly if this set of assumptions is not working for you.

Very often, we hold on to beliefs and assumptions that don't benefit us, that limit us, and that affect the way we walk in the world because they are familiar, a known quantity. We hold on to them because they are all we have ever known. But, most importantly, we hold on to them because we believe them to be true. And this is where we fall.

Know this:

**You are free to discard beliefs that are no longer working for you. You are free to adopt a new set of beliefs that actually benefits you. You are free to reinvent yourself and tell a new story. All of this is within your power, as part of the free will that Allah (swt) blessed you with.**

Remember, it's all available.

If a belief is not working for you, if it is holding you back, be brave enough to admit it – and then do the work to change that belief to something more positive, more nurturing, more useful to you as you show up, authentically and sincerely, in your life.

> REFLECTION: Which of your long-held beliefs are, in fact, limiting your potential?
> And what will you do to change them?

A transformative exercise that LaYinka asked us to do in one of her workshops may be helpful to you: write your limiting beliefs down in the past tense. As though it is something you have moved on from. As if it is something you have grown out of. As though it is something you no longer hold to be true.

*"I used to think I was a bad mother..."*
*"I used to think we would never be happy together..."*
*"I used to think I had no time to memorise the Qur'an..."*
*"I used to think I would never accomplish anything..."*

Now, how does that feel? Don't you feel lighter somehow, liberated even?

You have a choice: hold on to the beliefs that are stifling you, or replace them with more useful beliefs that will propel you towards the person you want to be.

Just imagine how your life would change if you replaced just one of those limiting beliefs with an empowering one, and lived as if it were true.

Just imagine.

# STEP THREE: CULTIVATE GRATITUDE

*"And admit me by Your mercy into (the ranks of) Your righteous servants."* **(Qur'an 27:19)**

If being positive is a crucial step towards showing up more fully, then there is one vital ingredient that deserves to be examined more closely. And that is gratitude.

I believe it was gratitude that pushed me to make sujood when I got the news that my dear husband had passed away. Some questioned this action. Some thought I had gone mad. But I knew where that sujood came from. It came from a deep and overwhelming sense of gratitude that I had been blessed with those years in the first place. It came from an acknowledgement that this wonderful man had been on loan to me – and I was grateful to have known him, borne his children, laughed and cried with him.

This poem I wrote on the Eid after his passing reflects the sense of gratitude, even in the midst of the sadness.

*When she speaks of him*
*Her eyes light up*
*Still,*
*Her voice grows soft*
*Still,*
*The memories come rushing back*
*Still.*
*When she speaks of him,*
*The weight lifts:*
*There is joy in the lightness,*
*There is healing in the remembrance,*
*There is peace in the knowing*
*That he was hers,*
*And it was beautiful,*
*And that he was beautiful.*
*So that, like the sun in April showers,*
*Her smile breaks through the tears.*
*So much to smile for,*
*So much to be thankful for,*
*So much to live for*
*Still.*

Gratitude helped me heal after my husband's death.
Such is its power.

Expressing gratitude to Allah (swt) forces us to focus on the positives in our lives, on the little blessings, the barakah we often take for granted. Making this a habit offers numerous benefits, including helping you to shift your paradigm, tackle negativity and develop an optimistic, grateful outlook on life. In her book, *'Abundance Now'*, world-famous speaker and entrepreneur Lisa Nichols says, "If you want great things to come into your life, you have to *first* be overwhelmingly clear about the great things that *already exist* in your life. You have to give them your energy and attention."

Giving energy and attention to the good we already have allows us to show up gracefully, with serenity and poise. I think of my children: how much energy and focus do I put towards being grateful that they exist, that they are as they are, that I have been blessed with this amanah? And how would my parenting style change if I focused more on the gratitude and less on the nerves, the irritations and the stresses of being a mother?

How would such a change in focus change me?
How would such a focus change them?

We can ask ourselves these questions about every aspect of our lives: our relationship with ourselves, with spouses, children, parents, extended family, friends. We may also ponder the effects of gratitude on our work, our life mission, our life situation.

Again, I remind you of Allah's words: **"If you are grateful, I will increase you..."**

There is a relationship between how grateful we are and how much Allah (swt) blesses us. And if we, as Muslims, know this, we should embrace anything that will help us to increase in gratitude. This could include using a gratitude journal, reminders on our walls or on our phone, morning and evening rituals where we actively recall things that we are grateful for on a daily basis.

REFLECTION: How could you intentionally bring more gratitude into your life? What regular activities or routines could you incorporate to ensure that you are living in a state of gratitude and positivity?

## Life's Lessons

*Know that you will only learn life's lessons*
*By living*
*By loving*
*By listening*
*By learning to pick up the pieces that scatter when you fall.*
*Gather them together,*
*They are a part of you,*
*Dust them off*
*Shine them up*
*Make them yours through and through.*
*On this journey*
*All we have are dusty feet*
*Open hearts*
*And wise eyes*
*To help us see our way through.*

# STEP FOUR: HAVE COURAGE

### "Courage starts with showing up and letting ourselves be seen." Brené Brown

Sometimes, we think that, in order to have courage, to be brave, we must be fearless. But courage is when you do that thing that you dread, with hope in one hand and fear in the other. You carry your fear with you and you act *in spite* of it.

And this concept of courage can be enormously freeing. Embracing courage means that you don't have to deal with *all* your fears before you decide to show up: you take them with you and show up anyway.

And, again, we go back to tawakkul, reliance on Allah (swt). We may be afraid, we may be uncertain, we may not have all the answers, but we have a Lord who is All Powerful, All Knowing, All Seeing, capable of anything. And He is waiting for us to call on Him, ready to respond to our calls for help, for solace, for a way out or a way through. And, if we truly internalised that, we would find it to be an endless source of courage.

The Lord of All the Worlds has your back. What is there to fear?

Just look at the meaning of salatul-Istikhara, the prayer we offer when asking for Allah's guidance on an issue:

*O Allah! I ask guidance from Your Knowledge, And power from Your Might and I ask for Your great blessings. You are capable and I am not. You know and I do not and You know the unseen. O Allah! If You know that this (...) is good for my religion and my subsistence and in my Hereafter–(or said: If it is better for my present and later needs)– then You ordain it for me and make it easy for me to get, And then bless me in it, and if You know that this (...) is harmful to me in my religion and subsistence and in the Hereafter–(or said: If it is worse for my present and later needs)– then keep it away from me and let me be away from it. And ordain for me whatever is good for me, And make me satisfied with it.* (Bukhari)

Let's pause for a moment here.

We have asked for guidance and invoked Allah's Power, Might and Wisdom. We have asked for our affair to be blessed and made easy, or to be protected from it and for it to be replaced with something better. SubhanAllah.

We have everything covered. No need to fear: simply trust in Allah (swt) and jump. As Lisa Nichols says in many of her talks, "Don't wait for the fear to stop before you leap. Be willing to leap afraid."

I'll be honest with you: I have been 'leaping afraid' my whole life.

I was afraid to leave my home in Zimbabwe to study in London on my own.

I was afraid to travel to Senegal in search of answers about life and faith.

I was afraid to tell my dad when I converted to Islam.

I was afraid to put my story out into the world in *From My Sisters' Lips.*

I was afraid to be the first niqabi on British television and face the likes of Lorraine Kelly and Melanie Phillips.

I was afraid to take my children out of school and take on the responsibility for their education.

I was afraid to run my husband's company and take on the responsibility of continuing his legacy.

I was afraid to uproot my family and start a new life in a new country.

I was afraid to close a business that had run its course.

I was afraid to start a new business that put me in front of a whole new demographic.

I was afraid to tell my in-laws that I was getting married again.

I was afraid to tell my husband that I no longer wanted to be in the marriage.

But I did it all.

Because the fear isn't a reason to stop or press pause; the fear is a reason to lean in, to push through, because strength, wisdom and growth are on the other side. And I have always found this to be true.

Indeed,

> **The difference between those who languish and those who progress is that, while the former fear failure, the latter understand that failure is merely part of the process. It is nothing to fear. It is merely another lesson learned. And, if we truly accept that the eventual failure or success of any task is in Allah's hands, why should we fear?**

REFLECTION: What fears have been holding you back from showing up more fully? Have you ever had to 'leap afraid'? What did you learn?

# Facing Our Fears

**"What would you do if you knew that the things that you fear were nothing but opportunities for you to grow stronger in your faith?" Lisa Nichols**

So often, we are afraid of a future event: a failure, disappointment or loss that *may* result from this action we are contemplating. But the paradox is this: we do not know the future. It is unseen. But we spend so much time and effort imagining the worst case scenario that it becomes fact in our minds. We feed into it until it becomes a reality; an inevitability.

But the truth is that we are creating an illusion and behaving like it's true.

And it isn't.

It is literally a figment of our imagination.

What are some of the decisions you may be considering right now that could take you out of your comfort zone? Is it something as simple as deciding to start working out or making changes to the way you eat?

Are you considering a *hifdh* programme? Or quitting your job? Or homeschooling your children? Or taking a road trip across Europe? Or starting a business or charity? Or dropping out of the rat race altogether? Leaving the country?

Interestingly, there are different approaches to this natural tendency some of us have to imagine the worst case scenario. Timothy Ferris, a famous podcaster and author of '*The 4 Hour Week*' actually advocates following your brain down this particular rabbit hole and genuinely getting up close and personal with your fears. Define them and examine them in the cold light of day: how bad could it get? How could you repair any damage? What else could happen? What do you stand to gain? And what is it costing you to postpone action?

Or how about a reframe of fear itself?

Bestselling author Steven Pressfield offers this perspective on fear in the face of taking action: "Fear is good. Like self-doubt, fear is an indicator. Fear tells us what we have to do. Remember our rule of thumb: The more scared we are of a work or calling, the more sure we can be that we have to do it."

"Fear is not your enemy," says Lisa Nichols. "Fear is your friend."

And I tend to agree with her. A certain type of fear will keep you from becoming complacent.

Will keep you up at night working on an assignment.

Will get you up at 4:30 am to invest in your dream.

Will keep your forehead on the prayer mat, asking for Allah (swt) to guide your child. Will get you to try one more time at making your marriage work.

Will have you asking your parents for forgiveness.

Fear, particularly fear of loss, can be a powerful motivator.

**It comes down to a choice: what meaning do you choose to give fear?**

# Showing up as a CEO

For the longest time, I rebelled against the label of 'business owner'. I didn't feel that it was a good fit, even as I ran the SISTERS Magazine for ten years. As far as I was concerned, I was a creative: an 'ideas' person, a visionary. I couldn't be bothered with the ins and outs of business planning, meetings and profit and loss. To be honest, I didn't want the responsibility.

Isn't that a funny thing? So often, the reason we resist showing up is that we don't want the responsibility. And I didn't want the responsibility.

For a long time, that worked out fine for me. I partnered with other people who were happy to take care of the business side of things while I concentrated on the creative aspects.

Until Sulayman (*Allah yarhamuhu*) passed away.

Up until his death, my late husband had been building a marketing company in Egypt, a call centre with high level clients, its own building in Cairo, and over 300 employees.

Now, all of a sudden, without knowing anything about the business or how to run it, I was a CEO.

In ways that I still can't fathom to this day, I found the courage to step into the role of company director, six days after his death, and let the company know that we weren't going down without a fight, that this wasn't the end, that we were going to continue growing, continue building.

From the third week of my *'iddah*, I was going to the office almost daily, meeting with managers, looking over income reports, dealing with staff issues but, most importantly, helping a family mourn its founder. It was heartbreaking seeing these young people, who had seen my late husband as a mentor and father figure, struggle to come to terms with their loss. He had built them all from the ground up, shaping their ideas, igniting their imaginations and fueling their dreams.

I was a poor substitute.

But I tried my best to walk in his shoes. To do what I thought he would have done. Or the very best I could do.

*I opened your laptop today*
*For the first time –*
*Your son knew the password.*
*I didn't.*
*I was immediately struck*
*By how very full your life was*
*How active your brain was*
*How full of ideas*
*And phone scripts*
*And client letters*
*Your days were.*
*Days spent far from me.*
*We lived parallel lives:*
*Me with my work:*
*The children,*
*The home,*
*The writing,*
*The friends.*
*You, with yours.*
*Now I am forced*
*To inhabit that world,*
*To wear your mantle,*
*To step into your shoes.*
*They are too big for me,*
*Of course,*
*And they are not quite my style,*
*But I'll manage,*
*By His Grace,*
*To shuffle in them for a while,*
*Until my steps become surer*
*Until my feet find their pace*

*Until I'm walking, running, sprinting,*
*Ready to win this race.*

But it was hard and, somewhere deep inside me, I resented this new responsibility that took me away from my children during the week, into the belly of Cairo, through the traffic, into a war zone that was not of my own making, one where I didn't know the lay of the land at all.

I fumbled my way through, without direction, without vision, terrified of the possibility of failure and what that would mean for my late husband's legacy, for the company's employees, for me as a person. Until, one December, the words of two thought leaders in the business world altered my attitude.

The first was Brendon Burchard. I had been a student of Brendon's for a while, taken some of his courses, watched his videos. But it was a message he sent to his mailing list that hit the nail on the head. It was about truly owning the role of CEO in your life. Accepting the title, accepting the responsibility, showing up as a boss. Living, thinking, acting, not like a victim or a helpless pawn, but a boss.

Shortly afterwards, I happened to pick up Seth Godin's book, '*Linchpin*'. At the time, I hadn't read many business books and, to be honest, I am not entirely sure why I picked this one up. But I am so glad that I did because it was a complete revelation to me.

In the book, Seth spoke about the necessity of bringing the fullness of your personality and unique character to the work that you do. His main point was this: whether you are a waitress or a marketing professional, bringing your authentic self to work and serving like you mean it is the only thing that makes you indispensable in an increasingly volatile employment market.

Seth challenged me to become a linchpin; not just a cog in the wheel, but an irreplaceable part of my company.

Seth challenged me to show up, to show up authentically and sincerely, for the business and everyone in it. And it literally changed the game for me.

From that day forward, I plucked up the courage to start treating the company like my own business. I asked questions about the direction of the company, the culture I wanted to cultivate, the experience I wanted my employees to have. I began to initiate projects that aligned with my vision. I invested in my staff's wellbeing and intellectual development. I worked hard to create a positive environment that reflected my values and the legacy I wanted to leave behind.

I showed up. Not as a substitute for the company founder, but as the current CEO, the person responsible for the future of the company.

My decision to show up in my new role, with all the new challenges, opportunities and responsibilities, allowed me to shed the resentment and recommit to that life stage. No longer was I trying to run away and hide. I was ready to embrace the learning and the growth that I knew awaited me, as long as I let it in. And, underpinning all of this, was the belief that I had held ever since losing my husband:

**You can do this.**

Allah's promise is true: never burdening you more than you can bear.

If He brought you to it, He will bring you through it.

I knew that there was a reason Allah (swt) had given me this responsibility and I knew that, ultimately, the results of my efforts would come from Him. I just wanted to be able to say that I accepted the challenge and did my very best.

The experience of running a company in Egypt, with hundreds of employees, almost every single one of them a stranger to me, and having to deal with accountants, lawyers, tax issues and hiring and firing was as far out of my comfort zone as I had ever been. It was the hardest thing I had ever done.

And I have to say, looking back, it was probably the most transformational thing I had ever done. As a result of that experience, I grew in ways I never thought I would, I developed skills I never thought I would need, and I found a strength I never knew I had. All by Allah's grace.

And that is the crazy thing about tests and challenges: they are so often the reason for our development and growth as human beings.

### Our characters are forged in the fires of the frontline.

The time that you didn't get accepted by your first-choice university; and ended up at another university in which you blossomed far beyond anyone's expectations.

The time it didn't work out with that guy you were so in love with but who wanted a haram relationship; and you walked away with a greater sense of clarity, and a closer relationship with Allah (swt).

The time you were so ill that everyone thought that you were on the brink of death; and you recovered and came back from the edge with a greater sense of gratitude and focus.

The time you poured money, time and effort into a business

venture that didn't work out; and you were able to move on to your next project with a better understanding of what works for you, and where your 'zone of genius' truly lies.

Thwarted plans.
New responsibilities.
Changing paradigms.

REFLECTION: Think about your life. How many times have you found yourself going through a test and coming out stronger on the other side?

So often, we resist these challenges. We are fearful of them. We try our best to avoid them and, when we can't avoid them, we resent them. And we run away. We hide.

I know I did. I just did *not* want to be pushed so far out of my comfort zone.

Which brings me to my next point...

## The Comfort Zone & the Nafs

**"The lizard brain is the source of resistance."**
**Seth Godin**

The comfort zone is where everything is familiar, present and accounted for: safe. There are no surprises here, no serious challenges, no threats. The comfort zone is where many of us are prepared to stay, tucked up under the duvet, eating chocolate and watching Netflix. This is where many of us languish and, eventually, stagnate and fade away because the comfort zone lulls us into a false sense of security: all will be well, as long as I stay here, in ease and safety.

I often wondered why there are some of us who welcome change and challenges and are motivated by goals, plans and dreams, and those of us who avoid change and challenges due to the risk involved and the potential of a future failure. Why are some of us more adventurous and others more cautious? And why are some of us driven to fulfil our potential and others happy to settle?

Apparently, we all have the capacity for both sets of responses.

The 'lizard brain' is the part of our brain that is primarily concerned with basic survival. It is motivated by fear and loathing. According to Dr Joseph Troncale (*Psychology Today*), "It is in charge of fight, flight, feeding, fear, freezing-up, and fornication." The desires, basically.

It is as if the lizard brain is another name for the nafs – the ego – that selfish side of us that wants ease at all costs, that avoids extra effort, that is susceptible to whispers, and whims, and base desires.

## Check Your Nafs

The nafs is the source of resistance to change, to growth, to striving, because often, changing and growing doesn't feel good. It requires effort, it requires work, it requires striving against the desire to take the easy way out. It is, in effect, a *jihad* to get the nafs in check and do the right thing, in spite of the difficulties.

**To show up – to choose commitment over apathy, hope over despair, growth over stagnation – we must get our nafs under control and choose courage over fear.**

Because life – that glorious process of growth and change and joy and pain – begins at the end of your comfort zone. For while you remain in your comfort zone, you will never show up fully and authentically in your life and fulfil your potential. You will never find the courage and inner strength you need to truly fulfil your potential.

How do I know this?

Because, when we always play it safe, when we constantly avoid risk, we are avoiding pushing ourselves beyond what we already know. We are avoiding stepping out beyond the boundary lines we have drawn for ourselves. We are avoiding rippling the surface of the water. Which means that we will never surpass ourselves. We will never do better, or more, or more brilliantly than we did last year.

**Remember, the only person you should be in competition with is yourself, no-one else.**

So, if you claim courage and hold on to tawakkul, reliance on Allah (swt), you have nothing to fear. You put in the work, the results come from Him – guaranteed. Even failure is not something to fear: it is merely a learning experience that will teach you valuable lessons about yourself and about what works and what doesn't work as you strive to live your best life.

REFLECTION: Are you living in your comfort zone right now? What fears are stopping you from stepping out and pushing yourself to the next level? How many of those fears could you trace back to your nafs?

## STEP FIVE: EMBRACE FLOW

Your life situation, that is, the circumstances in which you find yourself, will not always be ideal. In fact, more often than not, you will find yourself facing challenges and obstacles, things that threaten to throw you off course. As I mentioned before, this is the 'sunnah' of life: you have either been tested, you are currently being tested or you are going to be tested in the future.

And these tests could be in any of the spheres of life: your spiritual life, your relationships with your spouse, children and other family members, your financial situation, your health and emotional wellbeing, your social circle, or your own career or life mission.

The tests you are facing could be bringing your world to a standstill or simply wearing you down, leaving you feeling lethargic and hopeless. Or perhaps you've reached the stage where you can't be bothered any more. You feel like giving up. Like just not being there anymore.

I will never forget the first time I simply wanted to disappear from my life altogether.

It was Ramadan and I was alone in Egypt with the children. Their father was in the UK on business and the stress was starting to get to me. But it wasn't the lone parenting that had me rattled. It was the fact that it was Ramadan, a Ramadan I had planned for, meticulously: Qur'an reading schedule, du'a list, daily checklist, kids' programme, you name it, I had it figured out.

But my children were having none of it. They resisted and pushed back and, when they did go along with my plans, it was with reluctance. And I despaired.

Where did I go wrong?
Why don't my children love Ramadan?
Why don't they love the deen?
Why don't they love Allah (swt)?
What have I been doing all these years, wasting my time?

My brain couldn't reconcile the vision I had created in my mind – a vision of family harmony, a house alive with prayer and dhikr and peace in every heart – with the reality: a frazzled mum, on her own, trying to drag her kids to the masjid and losing her temper, left, right and centre.

Something inside me snapped.

I remember thinking at the time: '*I don't want to be here. I don't want to do this anymore. If this is my life, I don't want it*'.

I had reached my breaking point.

Maybe you've reached your breaking point before.
Maybe you've looked at your life and thought, 'Nah...'

It happens.

In spite of all that we know about patience and trials and tawakkul and trust, it happens. As shameful and ungrateful and *awful* as it is, it happens. There are those moments when despair grabs hold of us and threatens to pull us down into the abyss.

For me, these moments occur when I compare myself to what I think I should be, what my relationship should look and feel like, what my life should look and feel like. And that gap, that chasm, is too wide for me to bear sometimes.

> Reflection: When do those moments occur for you?

A sister wrote a piece in response to a prompt in our writing group. The prompt was:

*One day, she just walked away.*

This sister wrote a long and detailed piece about walking out on her family, her husband and her children, and getting on a plane to an unknown destination. The writing was raw and heartfelt and you could tell from the flood of comments that it resonated with so many of us.

For there are times when you don't just want to hide; you want to run away.

So, how do we resist the urge to escape and choose to show up instead, even when things are not how we want them to be?

The answer is simple:

**Learn to flow.**

# Seize the Day

**"If you survive till the evening, do not expect to be alive in the morning, and if you survive till the morning, do not expect to be alive in the evening, and take from your health for your sickness, and (take) from your life for your death."**
**(Ibn 'Umar, quoted in Bukhari)**

Human beings are so strange.

When we were children, we dressed up and pretended to be grown-ups.

When we were teenagers, we wished for the freedoms of adulthood.

When the responsibilities of adulthood dawned on us, we longed for the companionship of marriage.

When the pressures of marriage assailed us, we prayed for the arrival of a baby.

When the hardships of pregnancy manifested, we wished for the birth of the baby.

When the demands of weaning, potty training and the 'Terrible Twos' wore our patience, we wished for preschool.

Then we wished for the independence of primary school and we got the school run, homework, and school bullies.

Then we wished for the independence of high school and we got the hormones, the attitude and the anxiety of bringing up young Muslims in today's world.

We wished for them to grow up, for them to stand on their own two feet, for them to get settled and we got the empty nest, the secondhand marital drama and the uncertainty of middle age.

In the depths of the madness, or the loneliness, or the frustration, it can be so easy to wish for this particular life season to pass and for us to move forward into the next; one that promises more ease, more joy, more fulfilment. We spend each season wishing for the next. But the reality is, that season will come with its struggles, too. It will have its own tests, its own trials, its own challenges.

How do you know when you are wishing your life away?

One way to know is this: if you catch yourself saying, "I can't wait until…" you are likely not fully present in your current reality. That phrase – and the sentiment behind it – indicates frustration and dissatisfaction with your current life stage. It indicates that you would like to fast forward, that you expect happiness and ease 'once this is over'.

But, really, it is a matter of perception. If we see each life stage as merely a period to be endured while awaiting fulfilment in the next, we cannot show up fully in our lives as they are *right now*. We cannot be intentional, or mindful, or joyful because we 'can't wait for this to be over'. And we miss the beautiful moments. The moments that will never come again. Because the gifts of a season are very often specific to that season.

You will never be an adolescent again.
You will never be a new first-time bride again.
You will never experience your first pregnancy again.
You will never experience your first labour again.
You will never see your baby smile for the first time again.
You will never see your child take their first steps again.

All of life's firsts will fly by, never to be repeated. Those firsts will be replaced by new firsts and over and over until the end of your days. You will never get those firsts back.

So, cherish them.

One of my favourite expressions is 'Carpe diem'. Seize the day. Live each day like it's your last and wring every bit of goodness out of it.

Live your present reality and cherish it for the opportunities for growth and reward. Because each life stage comes with its own set of challenges but also its own set of rewards. Each stage invites us to show up, but show up in a different way, depending on the stage. Some of us may find some stages easier, or more enjoyable than others, but the opportunity for reward and connection and fulfilment are there, even in the stages that we find harder or more challenging.

Take a rather extreme example: the *'iddah* after the death of a spouse. One could easily tire of the state of mourning, the restrictions and expectations. One could easily wish this time away. "I can't wait until this is over." But then you would be missing out on the opportunity for reward, connection and fulfilment that is unique to that stage.

I will never get my *'iddah* back.

Even if I were to lose a husband again (*a–udhubillah min dhalik*), I will never get my first *'iddah* back.

So, take the time you've been allotted to heal, to reflect, to strengthen yourself, to let go. And emerge from that stage, knowing that you did all you could to show up in that season, authentically and sincerely and that, whatever reward was available in that season, you did your best to secure it.

**Just as there are challenges, there is beauty
in every life stage.**

What is upon us is to show up: to recognise that beauty, celebrate it and strive to be our best selves in that moment in time.

And be patient with every stage…

# Be Patient

It is worth noting that nothing worthwhile can be achieved without patience, nothing.

To be patient is to persevere, to put in the work and be prepared to see the results later, to stick to the plan even when the payoff seems distant.

That's how you memorise Qur'an. That's how you learn a new language. That's how you write a book. That's how you plan an event. That's how you start a business. That's how you raise money for charity. That's how you get fit and strong. That's how you raise a family.

**That's how you do pretty much anything that is worth doing: by being patient and putting in the work.**

Prophet Ya'qub's words in the Qur'an are a poignant reminder: *"Verily, patience is beautiful."* **(Qur'an12:83)**

And there is something beautiful about understanding that it's a marathon, not a sprint. That we are planting seeds, all of us, and seeds take time to grow.

So, in your journey towards showing up more fully in your life, remember the art of patiently persevering and be assured that the results are in Allah's hands. If you have a good intention and you show up to do the work consistently, diligently, you will see the results, by Allah's grace.

**Let go of perfectionism and of how you think things *should* be. Embrace the beauty of what is. Accept your reality and what that reality requires from you right now.**

Because life is a series of seasons and each season requires something different from us, just as it does in the natural world.

The season of preparation.

The season of sowing.

The season of reaping.

The season of rest and renewal.

Understanding life as a series of seasons is empowering because it indicates flow, movement: we are not static and our life situation is not static. We are in a constant state of movement. And the demands of one season are not like the next, just as the blessings and opportunities of one season are not like the next.

And that is why flow is so important. Rather than holding on to a fixed idea of who you are or who you were meant to be, understand that:

**Life requires us to be like water: flowing, abundant, and bringing good wherever we go, into whichever stream or valley or lake or sea we happen to find ourselves.**

For, just like the water that begins as snow, high up in the mountain, crisp and pure, that melts and starts trickling down towards the forest stream, then into the river below and on to the sea and wide, wide ocean, we too will go through different life stages. Stages that will change the focus of our lives, that will mould us, that will require different strengths and skills from us. Being flexible and embracing seasonal change are both vital to our ability to show up.

> REFLECTION: What season are you in right now? And how do you need to show up in that season? Are you ready to embrace the joys and challenges of this season?

I will never forget a sister who came up to me after an event and said, "Sometimes, I feel so upset that I am not able to be as active as I used to be, and be involved in da'wah work in the same way as sisters like you."

I asked her, "Sister, what is it that is stopping you from being 'active'?"

She replied, "I have four children that I am homeschooling." I gazed at her in wonder. Didn't she see what I saw? I took her by the hand and looked into her eyes: "Sister, you are 'active', ok? Don't ever let anyone tell you otherwise. You are doing sacred work here, important work. Please don't ever compare yourself to any other sister who is in a different position to you and blame yourself for 'doing less'. You just do the very best that you can with those children that Allah (swt) has blessed you with and enjoy this stage in their lives. Sooner than you think, they will have moved on and you will be able to be 'active' in different ways, maybe the ways you always wanted to be active in. Until then, give this life stage you are in, its haqq, give it its right: your focus and attention."

And therein lies the beauty of flow:

**You are able to bloom wherever you are planted and bring the beauty of your petals and the fragrance of your gifts to whoever needs them at that time.**

I invite you to consider another example: your relationship with your spouse. You probably started out on your marital journey with a truckload of ideas on how a marriage should look, sound and feel. And maybe it felt like that for a while – until the first pregnancy or the first child came along. All of a sudden, there was a shift (or maybe it was more gradual). You were no longer two lovebirds, with all the time in the world to devote to each other; you were now parents of a young baby, with everything that entails. This impacted your relationship in ways that may have felt uncomfortable. Maybe you blamed yourself when you no longer had as much time to devote to your relationship, or didn't look after yourself like you used to, or simply for the fact that you were tired all the time and just not that much fun anymore.

When this shift happens, it is easy to fall into despair, fearing that we have failed due to not living up to a particular standard we are holding on to.

But life happens. And it happens to the best of us.

**The point is that we choose to show up and remain intentional and positive in every life stage.**

The amount of Qur'an you are able to read and memorise while you are a student still living at home may not be the same as when you start work, are newly married or have three little ones under five.

The mother you are when it is your first child and everything is brand new and they are the centre of your world may not be the mother you are when there are four of them and you are juggling different ages and stages and the pressures of running a home.

The friend you are when you are single and independent and available at all hours may not be the friend you are when you are in the middle of starting a business, studying or building your career.

Be okay with that.

If you remember to be intentional, positive and courageous in every stage of your life, you will find that you continue to show up: to be a light and make a positive impact, no matter how large or small your circle of influence becomes. Because even the circle of influence is in a state of flux: at times, it will widen, at others it may narrow. Your job is to continue to shine, regardless, all else is in the hands of Allah (swt).

This is where the flow comes in. This is when you hold on to trust, to tawakkul, and accept that this is your reality *right now*. Yes, right now. This is not a life sentence. There is reason to believe that this, too, shall pass. That the ease is coming. That the dawn is near.

So breathe. And be like the water that flows.

And remember the promise of Allah (swt): **"Allah does not burden a soul more than it can bear."** Fact.

The more you believe that, the more firmly you hold on to that, the more you ingrain that in your consciousness, the more you will flow with the ups and downs of your life's journey.

Remember what we said about confidence leading to poise? This is the essence of flow: remaining serene and confident that you can overcome any trial, with Allah's help. That you have His protection. That there is good in it for you. That you are not here for a life of ease; you are here to learn and grow and become a better version of yourself. And the only way you will do this is if you ride the waves and stay on the board. And, if you fall off, clamber back on and keep surfing. You know what I mean?

# Settling

One last thing here. A sister read this chapter and challenged me: all this talk about flow and serenity, isn't that just settling? Isn't that the comfort zone?

My answer is this: you know when you are playing small and hiding, no matter what stage of life you are in. You know when you are scared or lazy or making excuses to avoid pushing yourself to the next level, whether that be in your worship, your exercise routine, the way you discipline your children or how much time you spend studying for your next qualification. You also know when you are stretched to capacity, when you are doing the best you can and can do no more.

This is the time to have an honest conversation with the woman in the mirror. Because you both know the truth.

**If you are hunkering down in the comfort zone,
you know.
And if you are capable of more, you know.
And if you are at capacity right now, you know.**

So, we need to be our own best friend: kind and confident, firm but fair.

Because the only person we should be competing with is ourselves. But we can't truly show up as our best selves if we aren't honest about where we are *now*.

*Isn't it strange
That we love
Although the promise of loss
Is ever present?
Isn't it strange
That we hold
Although the threat of separation
Is always there?
Isn't it strange
That we birth
Although the inevitability of death
Is a constant
Constant
Reminder?
Isn't it strange?
Isn't it strange
That our hearts can break
And heal
And break,
Only to heal again?*

*Scar tissue*
*Crisscrossing*
*Like embroidery,*
*Holding it together,*
*Just like we hold it together,*
*Just like He holds us together.*
*Aren't we strange?*
*Aren't we strange...*
*And wonderful?*

# STEP SIX: BE YOU!

I remember the moment when I first felt that I had lost my identity.

Having accepted Islam and now happily married, with a beautiful son, and living in a welcoming community, I still couldn't help feeling like I had lost myself. I looked at myself in the mirror and realised that I didn't know who I was anymore.

As so often happens when we get married and start having children, I had let myself go: physically, emotionally and mentally. I was on autopilot, going through the motions, doing what I knew I had to do, what everyone else was doing.

But did I feel like I was living to my full potential? No.

Did I feel passionate about my life and my purpose? No.

Did I feel like I was growing and learning and becoming a better version of myself? No.

I had settled into my comfort zone. And it showed.

You see, it wasn't meant to be this way. I had demonstrated a lot of potential in high school. I was an actress, prize-winning public speaker, Head Girl. When I left school, everyone believed that I was going to go on to do amazing things. I had 'star quality', they said.

But then, I became a Muslim, and everything changed. No longer the life of the party, I stopped drinking, stopped partying, started praying five times a day and put on a hijab.

"What a waste," everyone said.

As far as they were concerned, I had thrown away my life and, with it, all my potential.

And, in that moment when I looked at myself in the mirror and didn't recognise the woman looking back at me, I believed them.

Was this it? Was this all there was ever going to be? Was I not destined for something more?

So many of us find ourselves stuck in a rut, a daily grind that seems to go on and on and on. You feel like you're never doing enough, like you'll never measure up to other people's expectations. You wonder if this is all there is, for the rest of your life: this feeling of emptiness. This feeling of aimlessness. This feeling of disconnect.

I remember feeling that way once. Alhamdulillah, a lot has changed for me since that time. I believe it started when I started writing. Because the journey from getting my first children's book published to writing a bestselling memoir, and being featured in national newspapers and on TV, was a series of leaps of faith. Of doing things I wasn't sure I could do. Of saying yes when I wanted to say no. Of doing things I had never done before. Of pushing myself. Of challenging myself. Of leaving fear in the dirt and deciding to live a brave life.

I pushed back against fear to share my life story with strangers.

I pushed back against fear to be the first niqab-wearing woman on GMTV.

I pushed back against fear to speak in front of thousands of people about losing my dear husband.

I pushed and I pushed and I pushed – and I continue to push.

And none of this is because I am special. I am not better than you or any sister out there. I just made a decision, the decision to start showing up as my authentic self.

Every one of us has a gift to give to the world. Every one of us has something special to share. And that 'something' is yourself: your authentic self.

If you don't quite believe me and you're afraid to show up as your authentic self in case people judge you or laugh at you or try to shove you back in the box, practise these 3 habits:

- ◆ Be grateful for who you are. Open your eyes to your gifts, your talents, the way you are already showing up and making a difference, each and every day. And cultivate joy. Cultivate positivity. Cultivate intentionality. And, ultimately, cultivate gratitude for the gifts that you have been blessed with.

- ◆ Love yourself. You must. I know that no-one ever told us that growing up but now, we know how important it is for us to love ourselves, take care of ourselves and respect ourselves. Before you can ask that of anyone else, you must be prepared to do it for yourself. Stop comparing yourself to others; what others do, what others say, how others live their lives, how many Facebook friends they have, how they raise their children. Run your own race.

> ❖ Live with intention, every day. Be present, be mindful, be focused and purposeful. This is your life, to make of what you will. Yours to cherish, or yours to squander. Yours to appreciate, or yours to waste.

So choose to show up: honestly, authentically, with trust in the wisdom of the plan.

Show up as a woman.

Show up as a daughter, as a sister, as a wife, as a mother.

Show up as yourself.

# Lost

"I feel like I've lost myself."

I looked into the eyes of the sister standing before me. A pillar of the community, she was a devoted wife and mother as well a beloved teacher in a local school. And yet, she was not happy.

I asked her what she was doing to take care of herself, to fill her own cup. She looked at me blankly for a few seconds then laughed. "It's been so long since I did something for myself, I don't even know what I like anymore!"

It is not uncommon to find wives and mothers who feel this way. When your days and weeks and months are spent serving others, often without a break of any kind, it is hard to imagine doing something for yourself, for once.

The truth is, many of us grew up watching our mothers serve everyone but themselves. We watched our mothers sacrifice their dreams and desires for us, for the family, for the marriage. We watched our mothers take on everyone's burdens, everyone's worries, everyone's pain, seemingly without complaint. And we learned the lesson well: to serve is to sacrifice. To be a mother is to be a martyr.

Until we found ourselves walking, cooking, cleaning, caring in our mothers' shoes, we didn't know the meaning of exhaustion, of frustration, of isolation or resentment. We didn't know that, one day, we would look at ourselves in the mirror and barely recognise the woman staring back at us.

So many of us have been brought up to believe that there is only one way to be a good Muslim woman. That there is a mould and we have to fit it.

There is rarely an appreciation of individuality, or a celebration of the range of personalities and characteristics that Allah (swt) created us all with. Instead, there is a checklist and a list of preferred characteristics:

Docile

Quiet

Reserved

Domesticated

Obedient

Submissive

Shy

Passive

Followers

When it comes to life goals, there were only three important achievements: good wife, good mother, good hijab.

While there is nothing wrong with the above characteristics per se, it does cause a problem for those of us who are the opposite of those things.

Animated
Loud
Outgoing
Career-oriented
Opinionated
Independent
Confident
Active
Leaders

If you have ever been in a gathering of sisters and felt like you didn't fit in because you are just 'too much' or 'different', you will know what I am talking about.

Where did we get this idea that only a certain type of woman will be tolerated in the community? A woman who knows her place, who respects the status quo; a woman who doesn't rock the boat, who is happy to shrink and accept third and fourth place and put everyone else before herself.

Where did we get this from?

I have some answers.

Culture, often crafted to protect the interests of the most powerful in the community, must shoulder some of the blame. But we must also acknowledge that weak men (and women) have worked hard to preserve the status quo in favour of men's dominance and women's weakness. Thankfully, things are changing. Our perceptions of what is acceptable behaviour and personality for Muslim women is shifting, evolving, allowing us space to breath and find our own path, still in line with Islam, but also in alignment with how Allah (swt) made us.

But what does all this have to do with you showing up as yourself?

**Well, showing up as your authentic self may sound simple but, in reality, it is a bold statement of self-affirmation, of self-love.**

And no-one can love you until you learn to love yourself.

# Self-Love

No-one taught us how to love ourselves. Most of us grew up with criticism and comparison and conditional love as our constant childhood companions. Many of our parents, almost unwittingly, used shame and coercion as tools to mould us into the perfect daughter, the perfect sister, the perfect wife-to-be.

As a girl, you always had to measure up to so-and-so's standards: of behaviour, of looks, of potential. We never heard the words "You are enough". No-one taught us how to love ourselves. That was a lesson we had to learn as we walked as women. Some of us are still learning it.

But it is difficult to love yourself if you are still criticising yourself, still comparing yourself to others, still holding yourself to an impossible standard. There must be a balance between striving and acceptance. Between aiming for our highest potential and accepting our imperfections and loving ourselves in spite of them.

Because sometimes, the harshest critic is the woman staring back at you in the mirror. But that woman is also an amalgamation of every other person in your life, whose words you internalised and took into your belief system, from childhood until now. She manifests as your inner 'Mean Girl' and she is that voice you hear in your head that chants your limiting beliefs like *dhikr*, that repeats other people's criticisms and judgement, that tells you all the lies that you swallowed because you believed they were the truth.

You'll never be good enough.
You're an embarrassment.
You're a failure.

No matter how many times you've let yourself down in the past, no matter how many mistakes you've made, no matter how many times you have fallen, you have a choice regarding how you tell your story, how your internal voice recalls it. If you choose to be the victim, you will always focus on how you messed up, how it was ultimately your fault.

**If you choose to embrace the hero role, you will focus on what you did right, the good things that resulted from the difficult situation, how much you've grown.**

It is as if we forgot that Allah (swt) created us, beautiful in our imperfections, in our mistakes, in our failings, and in our ability to rise.

It is as if we forgot that Allah (swt) saw fit to bless us with talents and abilities, skills and knowledge and the ability to grow and progress.

It is as if we forgot that Allah (swt) created every one of us, absolutely unique, to fulfil our equally unique life purpose.

Some may wonder what is so unique about the purpose we were created for. Allah (swt) tells us in the Qur'an: **"I did not create the jinn or mankind except to worship Me."** **(Qur'an 51:56)**

Seems pretty straightforward, right?

But Oh, the beauty of worship in Islam!

How wonderful it is, what a *blessing* it is to have this holistic view of worship as a function of the heart, the mind and the body. To view worship as not just encompassing the ritual acts that we have been taught by the Prophet (pbuh), but countless daily actions that, done with the right intention, become worship, too.

Acts that you perform every single day, as a part of the roles you have been called to play. Whether you are a student, a boss, a mother, a wife, a carer, or a comforter, you perform tasks every single day that, with a change of intention, can become *ibadah* – as we discussed in the chapter on being intentional.

So remember that, no matter what your stage and what role you are playing right now, you have the capacity to show up as the hero, as the winner, as *you*.

# Allah Created You Unique

There is only one you. Throughout time, there has only been and will only ever be one you. Allah (swt) created you: uniquely gifted and full of the potential to achieve what you were sent here to achieve, to do what you were sent here to do, to be the hero of your own life story.

Your character, personality, background, life story and life circumstances are all unique to you: they make you who you are. Yes, even the trials and the failures and the setbacks. They have all moulded the woman you are today and that woman is stronger than you think, braver than you realise, capable of more than you can imagine.

Allow her to be.

Don't compare yourself to anyone else. Don't try to fit into someone else's mould. Don't try to change your character or personality to fit someone else's checklist.

**Be inspired by others but only in so much as their example encourages your light to shine brighter. Because your light is unique to you.**

REFLECTION: So now, you have a choice: are you going to be a copy of someone else, a shadow of someone else's experience and a follower on their journey, or are you going to be fearlessly you: with a unique voice, unique gifts, and a unique contribution to make?

# Find Your Tribe

*"It is sufficient honour for those who love one another for the sake of Allah, men and women alike, to know that their Almighty Lord will take care of them on the Day of Judgement and will say, 'Where are those who loved one another for My Glory? Today I will shade them under My Shade on the day when there is no shade but Mine.'"* (Muslim)

One of the many blessings that Islam has brought to my life is the joy of sisterhood, or female friendship. I spoke about this blessing at length in *From My Sisters' Lips* and I wish to reiterate it here, over ten years on.

I wrote then of Islamic sisterhood in the following terms: It is special. Founded as it is on the love of the Creator, it is a sisterhood without ego, without envy, without malice, jealousy or pride. It is pure and selfless. It transcends this world and it is beautiful.

I have been blessed to meet thousands of sisters since I first sang the praises of Islamic sisterhood and, like everyone, I have experienced the ups and downs of humans trying their best to embody Divine ideals. We don't get it right all the time, do we? Perhaps you have experienced pain or rejection or even heartbreak at the hands of other sisters. Maybe you have been the subject of gossip, rumours or smear campaigns. Maybe you have found sisters to be unapproachable or judgemental. Or maybe you have found that the majority of sisters are just not on your wavelength.

Whatever your experiences, I invite you to make a commitment to finding *your tribe*.

"What is my tribe?" I hear you ask.

Your tribe is the sisters that get you, that lift you up, that support you and help you to grow, as a believer and as a human being. You have the right to choose who you share your time with, who you confide in, who you turn to when you need a confidence boost, a sounding board or a good cup of tea.

**Find your tribe.**
**They are out there: the sisters who think you**
**are amazing, just as you are, who cheer you on and**
**hold space for you when you're trying to figure**
**everything out.**

Find those women and cherish them.

**And be the sister, the friend, you want to see.**
**Embody the traits that you are looking for in a sister;**
**make them a part of who you are.**
**And commit to sharing your light with those**
**who will help you shine, not those who feel**
**threatened by it.**

Take stock of the company you keep and how it affects you. Ask yourself the following questions:

- How do I feel when I spend time with this sister?
- Do I feel good about what we talk about and do together?
- Am I earning rewards when I am with her, or the opposite?
- Do I feel seen, heard and supported?

- Can I trust her?

- Will she pull me up if I am out of line?

- Have I grown as a result of our relationship?

- Do I love her for the sake of Allah (swt)?

REFLECTION: Imagine one of your friends asking herself these same questions about you: what would her answers be?

## How will you show up?

There is a reason I keep bringing the conversation back to you, O reader. And it is this:

**You only have control over *yourself*, no-one else.**

If you are not happy, what part have you played in making the necessary changes in your outlook and in your circumstances?

If your marriage is failing, what part have you played in understanding the causes and changing your behaviour and the way you communicate?

If your children are unsettled and acting up, what part have you played in getting to the root of their issues and helping them solve them?

If your business is faltering, what changes have you made to your mindset or strategy to get it back on track?

If your friendships are shallow and unfulfilling, what part have you played in finding your true tribe?

If your community is divided, what part have you played in uniting it?

In other words, in whichever part of your life that is not living up to its full potential, *how are you showing up?*

Don't talk to me about your childhood or the people who hurt you. Don't talk to me about your husband and how he doesn't listen and will never change. Don't talk to me about your children and how they don't respect you. Don't talk to me about your business and how hard it is in today's climate. Don't talk to me about your friends and how they are jealous and spiteful. And don't talk to me about the problems in your community.

I'm going to put it bluntly: all these are tests, plain and simple. They are obstacles along the way. Just like the obstacles that the hero encounters in the storybooks.

**Allah (swt) chooses our obstacles, our tests. We don't get to choose the tests.**
**But we get to choose how we respond.**
**And that is the most liberating and empowering belief of all.**

*We get to choose.*

Will we be the victim of our circumstances? Or the victor?

Will we hide behind our fears, doubts, excuses and blame, or will we show up, as our true selves, as our authentic selves, as the heroes.

When I speak like this, some people think I am being over-dramatic: after all, we all go through tests, right? We are all merely human beings, trying to make sense of things. We're not in control of our destiny.

Well, I choose to see it differently.

## My Life, the Masterpiece

I believe that my life is a masterpiece. While, in the big scheme of things, when you take into account the universe, the planets, and the billions of people that populate this planet, I am insignificant, I know that I am a miracle, too.

But Allah (swt) is capable of encompassing both realities.

I came to this realisation during the hajj. With thousands upon thousands of pilgrims all performing the rites and rituals, it is easy to recognise your own insignificance as an individual.

But, at the same time, Allah (swt) hears *your* du'a – and it is precious to Him.

**So, even in the midst of that sea of humanity, your whispered words have worth. Not only do the words and prayers have worth, but your heart has worth, to the Lord of All the Worlds.**

Think about that for a moment and marvel at this truth.

At once insignificant and a rapturous miracle.

That is how I choose to see my life: Allah (swt) chose everything about me, and for me and He continues to guide me, test me and send me signs. Me, this insignificant human being full of sin. He continues to bless me with new insights, people to serve, and opportunities for growth and reward.

And He does the same for you. All day, every day.

So what is stopping you from treating your life as the masterpiece it is, as the heroic journey it is?

If we are all simply on a journey back to Allah (swt), isn't it marvellous the many routes He plans for us?

**And so, if you will accept my premise that you are a masterpiece and that your life is a journey, you get to decide the role you will play in the story:
victim or hero.
You get to choose.**

And, if you choose to be the hero, know that all that is required is for you to show up, ready to win. Ready to learn, ready to grow, ready to repent, ready to serve, ready to shine, ready to succeed.

Because Allah (swt) is always working in your favour, even when it doesn't feel like it.

And when you know that, you know that you are already equipped with what it takes to show up as the hero, that all you have to do is claim the identity and trust that Allah (swt) has your back.

And the rest will take care of itself.

# NOTES

# NOTES

# In Conclusion

At the beginning of this book, I called showing up a 'Prophetic Sunnah'. Do you now see how he perfectly embodied the traits I share in this book: sincerity of intention, positivity, gratitude, courage, flow and authenticity?

Do you now see that all you need to do is decide to step up to the plate, to take on the challenges that Allah (swt) has set for you, knowing that you've got what it takes to prevail, that He has your back, and that you are destined to be the hero?

Every one of us goes through trials. Heroes are no exception. Think of the stories of the great women of Islam: Khadijah, A'isha, Asmaa, Fatimah.

Not one of them had it easy.
Not one of them got a free ride.

Instead, they were constantly tried and tested.

Divorce
Widowhood
Barrenness
Poverty
Injustice
Loss

And yet, we don't remember them as victims, as martyrs.
We remember them as heroes.
You are no different.
Choose to show up.

**And be the hero you were born to be.**

# A Final Visualisation

Imagine being surrounded by your children and grandchildren, telling the story of your life...

What stories will you tell?

Will you share the lessons you learned, the obstacles you overcame, the wisdom you have gained?

Will you share how you grew through adversity, always relying on Allah (swt)?

Will you share how, even when your faith wavered, you knew that Allah (swt) wanted good for you?

Will you share how, in your darkest moments, you knew, deep inside, that this was not designed to break you.

**That this life was not designed to break you, but to fashion you into something more beautiful, more resilient, more heroic, than you could ever have imagined.**

Will you show them how to be heroes in their own lives?

How to rise after they fall?
How to call on Allah (swt)?
How to trust in the process?
How to believe in themselves?
How to be heroes?

I know you will, insha Allah.

Go to **www.naimarobert.com/showup** to download an extended audio version of this visualisation exercise

**May Allah (swt) bless your journey towards being the very best Muslimah you can be and making the contribution you were born to make.**

# NOTES

# Acknowledgements

Above all, I thank my Lord, Allah, for everything that He blessed me with that made this book possible.

To my whole family for their support and encouragement: from my father, Robert McLaren and my sister, Gugu McLaren–Ushewokunze, to my children, Ubaid, Adam, Maryam and Amani.

Shout out to Mr Mightly for putting up with the long nights and absent wife while I worked on this book.

To my girls who were in the trenches with me as I wrote this book, LaYinka Sanni, Barakah Hassan, Elisa Damaliti and all the other amazing sisters who inspire me every day.

To the ladies on my team, Hend Hegazi, Fatima Mookadam and Raheemah Odusote, who were my first beta readers.

To my agent, Sheri Safran, for always fighting for me and being in my corner.

To Haris Ahmad, head of Kube Publishing, for believing in me and trusting that I would deliver.

To Yosef Smyth who was unfailingly supportive – you are missed!

To my editor at Kube, Asma Anwar, who totally *got* this book and did an amazing job on it.

To Jannah, the cover designer, and all who voted for their favourite cover!

To the thousands of sisters around the world that I have had the pleasure of connecting with, training and coaching; the Be The Hero readers, students and the Show Up Club family: you ladies made this book what it is. It is yours!

# Appendix: Bonus Material

Salaam!

This is your sister, Na'ima B. and I am so delighted that you chose to buy this book.

A small request:

- Go to **www.naimarobert.com/showup** and download the workbook that accompanies this book
- Take a selfie or picture of the book and post it on social media, tag me @naimabrobert and use hashtag #showupbook
- Write a review and post it on Amazon and Goodreads
- Suggest the book at your local book club and invite me to speak to your members!

# Join my free Show Up community online
# www.naimarobert.com/showupsisters

Access the free video and audio bonuses that I have created especially for my online community.

Meet other readers and share your takeaways, comments and reflections.

Get ready to SHOW UP like never before – with an amazing group of likeminded women at your side!

To join our community please go to
**www.naimarobert.com/showupcommunity**

APPENDIX: BONUS MATERIAL

# Redeem your Show Up
# Workshop ticket (worth £197)
# www.naimarobert/showupworkshop

I would like to invite you to attend my Show Up Workshop as a complimentary participant.

This dynamic workshop is designed to bring the six steps described in the book to life with real-life examples, case studies and practical tips for truly showing up in every aspect of your life.

This offer is open to anyone who purchases a copy of Show Up: A Motivational Message for Muslim Women.

To register and get more information, go to
**www.naimarobert.com/showupworkshop**

# Work with me
## www.naimarobert.com/coaching

I love working with women to help them build their confidence, find their voice and get to their next level, as their coach, mentor and cheerleader.

If you would like to know more about working with me, visit **www.naimarobert.com/coaching** and let's have a conversation!

# Bibliography

Brené Brown, *The Gifts of Imperfection: Let Go of Who You Think You're Supposed to Be and Embrace Who You Are* (Hazelden Firm, 2018).

Hal Elrod, *The Miracle Morning: The 6 Habits That Will Transform Your Life Before 8am* (John Murray Learning, 2017).

Timothy Ferris, *The 4 Hour Work Week: Escape the 9–5, Live Anywhere and Join the New Rich* (Vermilion, 2011).

Seth Godin, *Linchpin: Are You Indispensable? How to Drive Your Career and Create a Remarkable Future* (Portfolio, 2018).

Lisa Nichols & Janet Switzer, *Abundance Now: Amplify Your Life and Achieve Prosperity Today* (Harper Collins, 2016).

Steven Pressfield, *The War of Art: Break Through the Blocks and Win Your Inner Creative Battles* (Warner Books, 2003).

All of Na'ima B. Robert's poems were originally published in *'Four Months and Ten Days: Poetry & Prose from the Iddah'* (Sisters Awakening Press).

LaYinka Sanni (www.layinkasanni.com).

Lisa Nichols, 'How to Turn Your Fear Into Fuel' *(Mindvalley)* https://www.youtube.com/watch?v=v19rDdIh_kY&t=280s

Joseph Troncale, Your Lizard Brain: The limbic system and brain functioning, *Psychology Today (website)* https://www.psychologytoday.com/gb/blog/where-addiction-meets-your-brain/201404/your-lizard-brain

# NOTES

# NOTES